This practical and insightful business book combines organizational frameworks with real-world leadership experience to deliver actionable guidance on organizational effectiveness. By translating complex concepts into accessible strategies through relatable anecdotes and visualization techniques, it remains engaging and easy to apply. A valuable resource for leaders and managers, it supports improved organizational performance through disciplined thinking, practical execution and sustainable effectiveness.

Dominic Blakemore
CEO Compass Group plc

The Effectiveness Edge is a must-read for anybody who is responsible for driving organizational performance holistically. Actionable insights and relevant experience from the authors help provide a coherent, practical framework for organizations to acquire an edge and thus sustain a competitive advantage.

Bharat Puri
Senior Advisor and Director at Pidilite;
Independent Board Director,
Tata Motors and Tata Consumer Products

Organizations are fundamentally messy and complex. This is the first time in my career that I have seen the subject of organization effectiveness unpacked in a way that senior leaders can genuinely make sense of it. It cuts through the seemingly intangible issues that quietly erode performance and provides a practical starting point for work that can have a meaningful, measurable impact on the bottom line.

A must-read for any leader seeking to understand and address the underlying drivers of poor organizational performance.

Emma Rose
Chief People Officer, Convatec plc

If you care about performance, this is a book you can't ignore. In a world of hyper-competition and constant change, this book makes a simple, powerful point: every organization runs on two systems – the formal (structure, roles, process) and the informal (relationships, trust, influence). High performing firms don't choose between them – they connect them, ensuring value flows through decisions, information and talent. Robottom and Loughlin make it clear this matters now more than ever. Real value now comes from how work actually happens – through collaboration, knowledge flow and adaptive problem-solving. They offer practical steps to move beyond the org chart and design for real effectiveness. Because most organizations don't fail on strategy or technology – they fail where value stops flowing. Robottom and Loughlin will challenge you to find it and support you to fix it.

David Henderson
CHRO Al-Futtaim Group, formerly Zurich Insurance, MetLife and PepsiCo

The Effectiveness Edge is a powerful, deeply human guide to uncovering the hidden costs that quietly erode organizational performance. It gives leaders a rigorous, yet practical framework to diagnose complexity, reset systemic patterns and unlock the full potential of their people and strategy.

Annemarie Durbin
Board Chair and Executive Coach/Mentor

The Effectiveness Edge incisively, and often humorously, pinpoints the factors that block organizations from performing optimally. Not content to just admire the problem, the authors skilfully explain how to apply their well-honed formula to tackle the most knotty of cultural and organizational issues. For leaders who want to bring their A-game, grab this gem of a book, absorb the learnings and 'go slow, to go fast' in your business.

Andrew Gibson
Senior Partner, QLM Search

The Effectiveness Edge provides you with a great way to look at your organization through the systemic lenses of organization effectiveness. It helps you identify and diagnose your untapped opportunities. The 3D-OE Framework stirs you to look at both your collective and individual organization dynamics that impact the overall effectiveness. That in-depth look helps you think through the right organization model harnessing multiple perspectives and grounds it with data. The book covers – in a very holistic yet practical way – all that you need to have in your toolbox when you're to embark on your next transformation journey.

Stephane Charbonnier
Independent Board Member;
Retired CHRO L'Oreal USA

This book stimulates leaders to look beneath the surface at what is shaping organizational performance. It encourages leaders to pause, reflect and engage in deeper conversations. In my practice supporting senior teams to define and deliver their strategy and purpose, I value its invitation to go beyond symptoms and notice the hidden forces that determine what is possible and unlock potential.

Elaine Grix
Leadership and Team Development Coach

Most leaders know their organizations are messier than the org chart suggests – what they lack is a way to see why, and where to start. Loughlin and Robottom offer exactly that: a practical, rigorous diagnostic framework grounded in the messy reality of how organizations actually work. What sets this book apart is the authors' willingness to look beneath the surface – at the frames of reference that shape what leaders can and cannot see. In doing so, they open a door that too few OE practitioners walk through: the recognition that organizational effectiveness is inseparable from the developmental capacity of the leaders seeking to achieve it. A valuable contribution for any senior leader ready to go beyond the quick fix.

Nial O'Reilly
Director, Harthill Consulting

I read this wonderful, accessible and informative book in one sitting. If you are interested in understanding how organizations really work – and anatomizing the components of successful, high-performing organizations – this book is for you. Whether you are a CEO, CFO, CHRO, Organization Development Practitioner or simply someone deeply curious about all things organizational, each chapter is awash with practical ways to make your organization perform better.

Samantha Rockey
Co-author *The Social Brain* and
Co-founder Thompson Harrison

As I read this book I found myself repeatedly thinking: *finally, someone has articulated what so many leaders experience but struggle to name.* So much of the book felt deeply familiar having had this type of discussion six months ago, last month or even last week.

In acquisition and transformation work, we are often intensely focused on execution and yet what quietly determines success or failure is often what sits beneath the visible plan. The 'go slow, to go fast' message particularly resonated as some of the most expensive mistakes happen when speed is mistaken for progress. I especially connected with the OE Spine metaphor – the idea that organizations need both structural stability and movement, with communication acting as the nervous system, is a powerful image. The conclusion reinforced something I strongly believe – organization effectiveness is not a one-off redesign exercise or a people initiative sitting adjacent to business strategy. It is performance work.

Karen Sinnot
Director of People Solutions, Experience and Transformation, Santander UK; Non-Executive Director at East Suffolk and Northeast Essex NHS Foundation Trust

Most leaders know something in their organization isn't quite working, this book helps you see it clearly. *The Effectiveness Edge* combines deep insight with practical tools to diagnose and tackle the systemic issues that quietly erode performance.

Zareena Brown
Chief People Officer, Admiral Group plc

Drawing on the authors' deep experience, this user-friendly guide demystifies the complexity of organizations and offers leaders a practical diagnostic tool to improve organization effectiveness.

Emma West
Leadership Coach and Non-Executive Director

Having worked with Vanessa, I have seen first-hand her ability to apply organization effectiveness to complex organizations and business challenges. Along with her co-author, Andrea Robottom, she brings that depth of experience to this book which offers clear, practical guidance on how to uncover, think about and address organization issues to unlock real commercial opportunities. A highly valuable read for senior leaders.

Nathan Adams
Chief People Officer, Lloyd's

This book reflects the very best of Andrea – it's insightful, straight-talking and deeply respectful of the realities of organizational life. She doesn't offer fashionable slogans or 'one size fits all' solutions; instead, along with her co-author Vanessa Loughlin she shares hard-won wisdom and a disciplined approach that helps you get underneath the symptoms and deal with what's really driving performance, complexity and culture. If you care about building an organization that works better for customers, colleagues and results, I can't recommend this book highly enough.

Faye Frater
SVP EMEAA & Global Corporate Functions,
Intercontinental Hotel Group plc

Vanessa Loughlin Andrea Robottom

The Effectiveness Edge

How Organization Effectiveness Unlocks Performance

First published in Great Britain by Practical Inspiration Publishing, 2027

ISBN 978-1-80576-028-3 (paperback)
978-1-80576-027-6 (hardback)
978-1-80576-029-0 (ebook)

EU GPSR representative: LOGOS EUROPE, 9 rue Nicolas Poussin, LA ROCHELLE 17000, France Contact@logoseurope.eu

Want to bulk-buy copies of this book for your team and colleagues? We can customize the content and co-brand *The Effectiveness Edge* to suit your business's needs.

Please email info@practicalinspiration.com for more details.

Practical Inspiration
Publishing

Contents

Introduction

This book is about money and fish.

A significant amount of hidden cost is tied up in knotty organization effectiveness issues – the kind that slip through the net and never show up on an Income Statement, lingering because they're complex and difficult.

If you are a CEO, Executive or Senior Leader, you will be used to spotting and solving issues that are getting in the way of productivity, profitability and performance. You will be doing this against a backdrop of profound shifts in the business landscape and undoubtedly your organizations will be facing ever-more daunting challenges that will hinder growth, erode revenue streams, drive up costs and unsettle employees. We've also noticed that organizations are suffocating under their own complexity – layers of structure and process that no longer make sense, initiatives that have proliferated like weeds and the general busyness that pervades organizational life.

Throughout this book, we've both drawn upon more than 35 years' experience working with organizations across the globe. We've seen first-hand how difficult it is to diagnose the true nature of issues that hold back organization performance. In this book, we share our proven approach, designed to give you an *effectiveness edge.* Our 3D-OE Diagnostic Framework™ will help you clear the way for your organization to do less of what doesn't matter and more of what does. This is where the fish come in.

The fisherman's tale[1]

At dawn, a fisherman laid out his stall and arranged his gleaming catch with pride. There were more fish than he could display, so he stored the excess under the table, meaning to deal with them later. He turned his attention to the customers gathering along the quay.

As the day grew hotter, the forgotten fish beneath the table began to fester. At first a faint odour spread through the air – then gradually, a sharp, sour smell lingered around the stall. People wrinkled their noses and turned away. The fisherman kept calling out his wares, absorbed in the business of selling his fish, puzzled that no one stopped.

By mid-afternoon, the stench was undeniable. Only then did he remember the fish under the table. He crouched down, checked on the fish he'd tucked away and realized they were spoiled. After he'd removed the rotten fish and washed down his stall, the air cleared and people returned.

Over the years we've seen this story play out many times because organization effectiveness issues are a bit like rotten fish tucked under the table – ignore them and they quietly fester but bring them into the open and you can unlock real benefits.

What is organization effectiveness?

Organization effectiveness (OE) is difficult to pin down because it's a label, a concept, a collection of disciplines and an outcome. It's no wonder it's generally misunderstood with several labels that are used interchangeably, but referring to overlapping concepts, such as: organizational development, organization design and target operating model.

Definitions of OE cover a broad spectrum of all the things leaders need to do to align strategy, structures, processes, technology and people to fulfil their organization's vision and strategy and ultimately deliver value to stakeholders. The problem is that typically these definitions are high level, skim the surface and don't really help you work out how to get started to uncover your rotten fish.

Organization effectiveness is a space that deserves the rigour of a discipline yet is too often treated as optional or keeps languishing at the bottom of the to-do list. It covers the full breadth of the business and builds on a range of disciplines with the behavioural sciences and psychology at its core.

Organization effectiveness is both an art and a science that deals with the untidy and uncomfortable realities of being human. In short, OE is wide-ranging and complex – you can't put a box around it and you can never say it's done.

With all this in mind, below we unpack what *we* mean by OE. Organization effectiveness is about the end-to-end alignment of all the tangible elements of your organization to your vision and strategy. We call these tangible elements Constructs and they include everything from your organization charts to your policies, your technology to your physical locations. Organization effectiveness is also about how people show up. We've used the label Behaviours because they are observable – how people act, speak or conduct themselves, especially in relation to others. We've included a more comprehensive list of Constructs and Behaviours in the Notes section at the end of the book.[2]

It has been established for some time that there is a relationship between Constructs and Behaviours and we need to address both to embed any kind of organization change. However, what is often overlooked is the long-standing theory that Constructs and Behaviours *hold each other in place* through the Interplay between them.[3] This is the crux of what we mean by OE: the strength of the interaction and influence of the Interplay. There is a deep reciprocity and ongoing dance between Constructs and Behaviours, and it is this Interplay that actually holds in place and perpetuates accumulated patterns in the system. This is why organizations are so hard to change. When OE is truly successful, Interplays shift – a reset occurs that loosens long held patterns which have been anchoring the organization in place, and allows new ones to form.

In summary, our definition is:

Organization effectiveness is when leaders are willing and able to optimize Constructs and influence Behaviours to shift and reset the Interplays that will generate the performance required to deliver strategic goals.

To bring this alive, imagine in Figure 1 that the Constructs are the weathered wooden uprights of an old pier. The sea birds perched on them are displaying Behaviours such as resting, preening and preparing for flight. The Interplay is the dynamic between the birds and those uprights: their habitual patterns shaped by the fact that the pier has remained unchanged for a long time. If most of the uprights were removed, this Interplay would shift; the birds would have to change their Behaviours to adapt to the new Constructs.

Figure 1. Seabirds on the old pier

Whilst a clear definition of OE is useful – it gives us structure, a shared language and a common starting point – we now need to step into the reality of how organizations actually work.

Organizations may appear to be straightforward and logical when they are depicted on an organization chart, but the nice lines and boxes hide their true nature. They are not neutral environments as they are really living systems that are messy, ambiguous, uncertain and sometimes scary. This is why, even when the costs are quietly piling up, we struggle to know where to start or we jump to interventions that often fail to achieve their intended outcome. People keep their heads down and think 'this too shall pass'.

If you are up for the challenge and you want the advantage of the effectiveness edge, you need to get below the surface to understand your OE issues using a proven methodology. To get the best outcome, you need to start with an OE diagnostic. It's that counterintuitive moment when you *go slow, to go fast*; pausing to accurately diagnose the true nature of your issues, before moving to solutions.

The Effectiveness Edge – the 3D-OE Diagnostic Framework™

We wouldn't go swimming in the sea if we hadn't assessed the swell, currents, rip tides or the weather and yet there is so much expectation on us to fix issues quickly before we've had a chance to understand the conditions. This can result in great ideas that don't fully realize their intended outcomes, fragmented approaches used as a way to make complex issues easier or simplistic solutions that simply skim the surface. More often than not we get expediency rather than effectiveness, and the illusion of progress rather than real change.

This book introduces the 3D-OE Diagnostic Framework™ which always gives you a place to start when facing knotty organization issues, regardless of your industry sector or type of business. The 3D-OE Diagnostic Framework™ is a versatile, adaptable approach that helps you unlock organizational complexity by accounting for multiple frames of reference and generating a genuinely three-dimensional view – up, down and across your system. Composed of an integrated Model and Process, the Framework provides the structure to gather, organize and shape insights by relying on deep listening and respect for colleagues' perspectives. Designed to be inclusive, it encourages people to get their 'fish on the table', begins the work of winning hearts and minds, and reduces the risk of quick expedient fixes that simply perpetuate stagnation.

We've split the book into three parts. Part 1 illuminates the hidden costs lurking inside OE issues. In Part 2 we dive into the Framework itself, brought to life with a marine analogy and anonymized case studies, blended from many organizations to keep things discreet. Part 3 shares our practical tricks of the trade so you can use the Framework confidently in your own organization.

Throughout this book we give you a way to put your 'fish on the table' and unlock performance.

Most organizations are ineffective. Yours doesn't have to be.

Part 1
The hidden costs in organization ineffectiveness

Chapter 1
The cost of our frames of reference

'The octopus is a stupid creature, for it will approach a man's hand if it be lowered in the water.'
Attributed to Aristotle[1]

We now know octopuses are curious, playful and intelligent creatures. Aristotle, the great thinker, philosopher and polymath was seeing the octopus through the limitations of his existing frames of reference. Consequently, he misunderstood the octopus.

What are frames of reference?

Frames of reference typically refers to the set of assumptions, values, experiences and expectations that shape how all of us interpret events, information or people. Throughout our lives, every one of us has absorbed a myriad of inputs and developed in our minds an interconnected paradigm we use to make sense of the world. It is this behind-the-scenes, mental structure that determines what we believe, how we think, and how we show up, react, respond and live on the visible stage of life. Our frames of reference can become fixed or can be adapted as we learn and adjust as we go through life.

Where do our frames of reference come from?

If we stick with the octopus for a moment, another thing we know about them is they lack receptors to perceive colour. Human beings also lack receptors for a different reason: we switch them off. This means we can't always discern the full materiality of what is really going on around us. We could think about this as the colour of a situation – its emotional tone, underlying mood, risk level and clarity. The reason that our receptors are switched on or off is due to our life-experience. So, let's explore a bit further how this comes about.[2]

In our earliest years, we absorb – almost without question – the beliefs, rules, judgements and cultural norms modelled by our parents or guardians. These shape what is considered acceptable within the family dynamic. We learn how to secure food and comfort, how to avoid upsetting those who care for us and how to attract attention when we need it. These early patterns of behaviour and understanding are passed from generation to generation, often without conscious awareness.

In adolescence, as we venture beyond our family, wider systems begin to shape us. Authoritative adults, teachers, school cultures and social relationships all influence how we see ourselves and the world. It's also the case that in recent years, social media has radically altered our sources of authority. Its reach is vast and anonymous, and it exerts influence that goes largely unchecked. Anyone can present themselves as an expert and broadcast opinions as though they were fact, regardless of whether they hold genuine expertise.

Throughout adulthood, our perceptions continue to be shaped and reshaped by relationships, work, politics, media and our own life experiences. Social media remains a powerful influence. By this stage, a considerable number of our beliefs, thought processes and behaviour have been formed in our early life. Whilst many of these remain highly functional, all of us carry mindsets that have outlived their usefulness. These mental patterns were often strategies that helped us survive our early years. If, as adults, we fail to recognize these patterns and our ability to adapt our thinking has diminished – like a muscle we don't use any more – our perspectives can become fixed in place as we get comfortable with them. These out-of-date ways of thinking can surface even when the present reality is very different from the one in which those patterns were formed. For example, we may unconsciously withhold trust from someone who resembles or behaves like a person who once caused us physical or emotional harm in childhood.

Over our lifetime we form our understanding of the world through the filters we've developed, shaped by the receptors we choose to engage or ignore. What we perceive feels true to us. Yet our perception is not the whole truth. It is simply our interpretation of what seems real, shaped by our own frames of reference. Each of us sees only part of the picture and others may experience the same events, situations and people in very different ways. This is why many large organizations emphasize the value of 'speaking the truth as you see it' – acknowledging that multiple truths can coexist.

Picking up on the influence of social media on our frames of reference, we're all aware that the amount of data we receive continues to increase exponentially. Large language models, commonly referred to as AI, are now a powerful force in our everyday lives. AI is creating, multiplying and accelerating the generation of data across the globe. The sheer scale, speed and variety of information coming at us cause a level of overload that no one can fully process. All this is taking place in the uncharted waters of a geopolitical context that continues to unfold. We experience this as rising complexity.

The endless stream of soundbites, opinions and updates hurled at us by friends, social media platforms and trusted sources means our attention is stretched thin. The pace of modern life leaves us little room to reflect. While our brains are remarkably receptive, biology demands that we filter incoming information to avoid overwhelm. One common coping strategy is to accept input at face value. Yet over time, if we fail to examine the flow of ideas, they can solidify into truths we simply absorb into our frames of reference, rather than perspectives we consciously choose.

In essence, our frames of reference are influenced by our family history and upbringing. Then our learned behaviour and the information we absorb develops through our life experiences. All of this influences what we choose to believe, our psychological make up and the way we decide to develop ourselves. We perceive unconsciously through our unique frames of reference and use them to make assumptions and judgements and to draw conclusions. These then result in the actions we take and the decisions we make.

The strength of the system

Organizations also have their own unique paradigms that shape our frames of reference as we come to work each day. These paradigms show up in the practices, ways of working, norms and habits of the organization we work for. The longer we stay, the greater the extent to which we internalize and embody our organization's paradigms. This manifests in many ways including what we are prepared to do or say, what we avoid or overlook and even how we present and what we wear. All this happens unconsciously. Organizations get under your skin. If individuals learn to operate through the organization's Constructs, then their Behaviours will gradually adapt so that they fit in with their colleagues and can be successful in that system. As this dynamic is repeated and replicated, organization-wide patterns of Behaviours are generated and perpetuated. It's these Interplays, between all the Constructs and all the Behaviours of all the people, that generates a living system.

Below are our top three characteristics of a system:

1. **Systems are like living organisms.** They are not conscious, but function like living entities. They respond to stimuli, grow and develop, maintain homeostasis, and adapt through evolution.
2. **Systems seek to survive.** There will be some paradigms that have evolved over time and become embedded because at some point they ensured the survival of the organization. As they are so deeply rooted, the system fights to preserve them.
3. **The system gets inside everyone in the organization**. You can see this phenomenon when new people arrive and see and do things completely differently. Then they slowly adapt to 'the way we do things around here'.

Assigning potency to something we can't see or touch might sound extremely odd, but we do it all the time when we talk about culture. Seeing the system as an entity in its own right may sound implausible. Yet if we are able to take this at face value, it is an extremely helpful perspective when seeking to understand what's going on in an organization. Choosing to take the system into account when attempting to change something is essential to unlocking OE. In essence, there is an invisible 'player' in the mix. It's usually ignored, yet it's the most powerful – the system itself.

Living systems hold lots of individuals with their unique frames of reference, all working together, generating and being influenced by the organization's paradigms. Added to this are the ongoing day-to-day pressures in organizations such as change, power struggles, hierarchy, conflict, inclusion, as well as external pressures and so on. With all this going on, we start to get a sense of why organizations can seem so messy. These are the conditions in which we are seeking to influence OE issues that will improve the performance required in our strategy.

What is the hidden cost?

Our frames of reference are going to be limited in some way. These limitations shape our behaviour. It's these Behaviours, coupled with the strength and messiness of the system itself, which lead to hidden costs.

To further illuminate limitations in our frames of reference and how they impact cost, we've taken inspiration from constructive adult development theories.[3] The various theories suggest that as adults, we evolve how we make sense of our experience over time and are potentially more able to handle complexity as we develop. If we continue to develop our sense-making capacity this leads to wider frames of reference and an ability to increasingly consider multiple perspectives. We may also stay quite comfortably at certain stages of our development for many years. However, this will impact how we spot and address OE issues.

We want to emphasize that this is not about pigeonholing or labeling individual people. We all have useful and limiting facets to our frames of reference. This is about becoming more aware of what's hindering our capacity, and how we may enhance it, especially in relation to OE.

Below we explore three common frames of reference and what happens when they have not been developed over time. We've seen these three frames of reference show up in all types of people, in all types of roles and in all industry sectors. They generate significant costs, especially if they show up in very senior leaders.

Conflict avoidance

We all know that positive relationships, team coherence and a sense of community contribute to a positive working environment and overall performance. Many leaders have the capacity to attend to relationships whilst balancing this against other outcomes that may be equally or even more important. However, when someone hasn't yet developed wider frames of reference and their focus on maintaining positive relationships is paramount, this can show up as avoiding conflict.

Avoiding conflict can result in Behaviours such as:

- Steering clear of handling poor performance.
- Shying away from decision-making unless everyone agrees.
- Poor meeting management.
- Appeasing those who shout loudest.

- Appointing people who don't challenge you.
- Spinning messages by selectively emphasizing more favourable information.

Let's take one example. Say there are two senior functional executives who have been friends for a long time. They find themselves in conflict with each other over a strategic decision. Due to concerns about damaging their personal relationship, the conflict remains unresolved. They are civil to each other in leadership meetings and they continue to get along on a social level. However, when they are leading their own teams, because they have taken opposing views to the business issue, they each continue to lead their people toward different outcomes. This shows up as disruption in the system including blocked initiatives, slower progress towards the overall strategic goal and people in key roles being stuck between a 'rock and hard place'. The senior leaders may be able to rationalize this state of affairs, but at the lower levels of the organization, over time, these rifts frequently create an 'us and them' split. There is confusion, frustration and anxiety and trust starts to be eroded. To get at the hidden costs, think about all the people attending unproductive meetings, all the swirling around conflicting priorities, all the projects that don't align, all the duplication and all the time spent on the post-meeting chat trying to make sense of what's going on. If you take only a proportion of the employment costs of every person involved or impacted by the unresolved conflict and multiply it by the time period, you start to get an estimation of the scale of the hidden costs – this is real money that is not being used to drive performance.

Blinkered specialist

No organization can function without specialist expertise. Expertise is vital in the development of products and services and in the day-to-day running of organizations. When leaders have wider frames of reference, they are able to apply their expertise in the context of the broader organization vision and strategy: they can see the bigger picture, they can appreciate and accommodate other areas of expertise and integrate different disciplines towards more comprehensive outcomes. However, when someone's frames of reference remain focused on their particular technical expertise, they can show up as inflexible, critical and blocking of unfamiliar or new approaches. They seem more concerned with being right within their discipline than the overall effectiveness of enterprise outcomes.

At a senior level we can all think of experts who become immovable because they can only see a situation from their own frames of reference and are unable to take into account the wider context. These leaders require significant effort to lobby and accommodate. This can delay progress or halt work on projects, require workarounds and typically creates high levels of frustration that spreads through the organization. We can apply the same formula to calculating the hidden costs as outlined in the example above.

At lower levels the scale of the hidden cost is still notable but may be even more difficult to identify. Think about the volume of reports that are written and never read, the use of expert language that generates more questions than answers or where processes become mired in red tape and have lost sight of delivering the outcome.

Goals at all costs

Statistically 57% of people in organizations worldwide are likely to have frames of reference that centre around achieving *immediate* goals.[4] People with this way of looking at the world have the potential to move mountains and are the backbone of all successful organizations. They focus on output delivery, innovation and efficiency. There is no doubt that experiencing the world in this way brings many strengths. Nevertheless, when leaders have developed wider frames of reference, they can leverage their drive and conviction towards the realization of *future* goals. As this development occurs, they usually become more aware of their strengths and limitations and so are more conscious of how they show up. As an example, leaders with wider frames of reference can see the value of different perspectives and take them into account, although they may still find this irritating if it slows them down or gets in the way of their goal.[5]

However, when peoples' frames of reference become too fixed on goals they tend to show up with a singularity of purpose that is so focused on what they want to achieve that other important perspectives are disregarded. Alternatively, they fail to adapt when circumstances change. They can show up as bulldozing, dogmatic, dismissive, unable to slow down and constantly driving actions. They may also value doing over thinking, output over outcome and tend to impose a relentless pace on their teams.

Pursuing any goal draws on valuable organization resources – people, time and budget. However, when a focus on goals becomes unwavering, we risk implementing simplistic or mis-aligned solutions that don't fully realize our intended outcomes and leave deeper challenges unaddressed. Solutions of this kind emerge when we stick to a goal at all costs even when circumstances change; when pressure from above demands visible progress; when inconvenient realities get in our way; when we are trying to tackle something genuinely complex too quickly; or when we fail to consider a broad range of perspectives including those with dissenting views.

When we are pursuing a legitimate goal, we will inevitably use organization resources. However, if the solutions are simplistic or misaligned, we end up spending money without getting to the outcome. These solutions can offer quick comfort and we may even realize a level of return on our investment, but the reality is more opaque. Costs hide in the illusion of progress: masking complexity rather than resolving it, fostering cynicism and creating repeated cycles of effort that continue to miss the mark. There is so much cost hidden in organizations because of these frames of reference – we've all been busy fools at one time or another.

Power and hidden agendas

There are two other features of our frames of reference that have a disproportionate influence on OE.

The first of these is power. We don't tend to think about it as part of our frames of reference. We tend to be more conscious of how power shows up around us in terms of who has power over us or whether we have power in the position we hold. It's really important that we are aware of our frames of reference around power because it can be exacerbated by the strength of the system we are in, the roles we take, the leaders we work for and the work we choose to do.

Earlier on we touched on the strength of the system and how the system itself gets inside you. In our experience, how power shows up in your system intensifies the frames of reference you already hold about power. To short-cut a complex topic, if you lean towards power as control and you work for an organization with a similar paradigm, you are more likely to behave in a controlling manner. If you incline towards power as responsibility and your organization reflects this, you are more likely to place emphasis on guiding and stewardship. If you gravitate towards the idea that power has the capacity to make a difference and the culture of your organization aligns with this, you're more likely to shape outcomes for yourself and others. Fundamentally, the frames of reference you bring *to* the system can also get amplified *by* the system as it magnifies the way you already look at the world.

How we perceive power will directly impact how we behave. For example, the levels of risk we're prepared to take, the degree to which we will collaborate and even whether we take accountability or not. In the context of the system we are in, this shows up as either enabling or hindering addressing OE issues. For example, we can leverage positional power to get in the way of noticing or sorting out OE challenges. When this happens, we effectively hide cost through an unexamined system or by maintaining the status quo. More on this in Chapters 2 and 3.

The second feature is hidden agendas. The three common frames of reference we explore above and the dynamics around power become all the more potent if there are hidden agendas involved. Hidden agendas occur in organizations when someone does not believe, in some way, in the vision and strategy of the business. They can also occur when someone is pursuing their own personal interests based on a deep psychological need. Hidden agendas foster unhelpful Behaviours, for example, sabotaging, failing to make timely decisions, obfuscating or manipulating.

Hidden agendas are complex psychological phenomena. Whilst some people will have some awareness that they are deliberately obscuring their intent, in general, people are not fully aware they are pursuing another outcome. They don't realize that their Behaviours are having such a significant impact on the effectiveness of the organization. When people show up with a hidden agenda they may be experienced at different times as charming, difficult to pin down or unpredictable.

Here are some examples of the Behaviours you might see when people have hidden agendas:

- Giving multiple people slightly different briefs.
- Sharing only part of the picture.
- Committing to work that's not fully aligned.
- Playing people off against each other.

All of these create unintended consequences in terms of OE issues and generate hidden costs.

Summary

Our frames of reference may keep us looking at the surface of our organization and obscure what's really going on. We all make assumptions, misunderstand and reach the wrong conclusions just like Aristotle. Without awareness of how our frames of reference impact how we see things, we will inevitably instigate and perpetuate hidden costs. We need to be *willing and able* to consciously see the reality of our organization.

However, with all this system strength and the muddle we bring as humans, it's no wonder it's challenging to see clearly into the murky organizational depths. The Greeks saw the sea both as a force of life and a source of chaos. Their great marine god, Poseidon, embodied this tension between order and mess. This is a useful notion when it comes to OE issues because, as a leader, you need to be willing and able to manage this dynamic. One of the most effective things you can do to bring more order and reduce the chaos is to become more conscious of your own frames of reference and the Behaviours that they drive.

Chapter 2
The cost of the unexamined system

'The unexamined life is not worth living.'
Attributed to Socrates[1]

What is an unexamined system?

When we think about our organizations, we often sense that something isn't quite right, yet struggle to pinpoint exactly what the issue is. Our individual frames of reference will be a factor, but this doesn't change the reality that OE issues are fundamentally systemic and complex. To understand the true nature of these challenges they have to be examined thoroughly – inspected in detail, thought about carefully and considered from every angle. Examining an organization means looking at issues that relate to or impact the system as a whole. Systemic issues are interconnected; they show up in patterns, relationships and underlying structures rather than in isolated problems. To get at them we really have to probe deeply and examine all the aspects of the situation.

As a seasoned leader, you will have your receptors switched on to recognize what is working and what isn't working in your organization. Nevertheless, the nature of OE issues remains elusive. If you think about an octopus, they have eight prehensile arms and hundreds of suckers which independently take in information from their surroundings. They are able to hide under rocks so you can't see them in their entirety; they can get their whole body into the tiniest crevice and once in there, it's virtually impossible to remove them due to the suckers. Additionally, with their incredibly versatile skin camouflage, octopuses are also extremely difficult to spot in the first place. When we do spot them, at first glance they often look like something they are not. Take, for example, the mimic octopus that impersonates the shape of around 15 different animals including a venomous sea snake and the spikey lionfish. Organization effectiveness issues are not dissimilar. They are hard to spot because they permeate all the nooks and crannies of the system, they often present as something different and they are hidden in plain sight by the relentless busyness of day-to-day life. We so often misunderstand their true nature. Once OE issues are embedded in your system they are hard to dislodge.

The ambiguous reality of organizations

Organizations by their very nature are ambiguous. Organization effectiveness issues, just like every other pressing commercial challenge, can be looked at in more than one way or interpreted with more than one meaning. With so many people viewing situations through their own frames of reference, hidden agendas beneath the surface and the constant pace and pressure of daily work, matters often end up unclear, poorly defined or incomplete. We also have a tendency to view situations as if they are static when in reality they are changing all the time. As organizations are living systems, decisions are made, new Constructs are put in place and people are continually being influenced to adapt their Behaviours. The organizational waters are constantly moving and these Interplays create ambiguity that prevents us from figuring out what is going on.

Let's look at two common aspects of organizations that create ambiguity and may prevent examination of the OE issues.

Fragmentation

In Chapter 1, we talked about the rising complexity we have to handle and the risk of overwhelm that this brings. One useful strategy we commonly deploy is to break things down into smaller elements. This is a well-known and proven approach and underpins many change methodologies. Yet, as complexity increases, we've seen our propensity to break things down, turn into fragmentation in organizations. Even when we try to join things up – for example, by implementing enterprise-wide technology systems – we can still end up papering over existing fragmentation or creating it in a different form. This shows up in organizational Constructs when, for example, processes are segmented or become a series of micro-specialized tasks, leading to multiple handoffs and widespread disconnects across the business. More broadly, across many sectors, fragmentation has led to a steady narrowing of role scope, the rise of functional specialists and the demise of accountable generalists. All of these Constructs impose constraints on peoples' Behaviours because they are required to stay within the confines of narrow roles. This can foster unhelpful divisions in the organization and prevent common sense decisions being made.

Over time, this kind of fragmentation may even narrow a person's frames of reference and create friction between people as they begin to interpret the world in a more restricted way. Overall, the resulting Interplay contributes to creating a systemic pattern of ignoring the whole and not joining up across boundaries. Taken to its extreme, over time this is likely to decrease the capacity of people to see the whole at all. Fragmentation gets in the way of leaders being able to examine systemic issues because they are trying to work with people who can only see things from a narrow perspective, limited to where they sit in the organization.

Ironically this propensity to try and simplify by fragmenting actually leads to more complexity. If this Interplay isn't addressed, an exponential doom loop emerges because every time complexity increases, leaders use fragmentation to try and solve it, which in turn increases complexity and so on. The work leaders have to do in order to make sense of OE issues by joining up increasing numbers of perspectives is like piecing together a jigsaw puzzle that used to be 500 pieces and is now 3000.

Surface level insight

As we start to examine our organization systems we are likely to begin by looking for information from which to generate insights to inform our decision-making. Insights provide deep meaning and understanding and fresh perspectives that can influence our frames of reference. What we will probably find is that there is a lot of raw data and stand alone, standardized reports, like organization health or engagement surveys, that tend to focus on tracking high-level themes. We may also find there are gaps in the data so that the nature of OE issues isn't fully illuminated. More often than not, information that could be useful to us may be discounted, used in isolation, misinterpreted, distorted by hidden agendas or vary in quality such that any insight we could glean remains elusive.

If we just look at two types of information we can start to see the problem:

- From an enterprise perspective, data comes from the Income Statement (sometimes called a Profit and Loss or P&L). This accounting source helps stakeholders evaluate financial health, spot trends and assess whether the organization is functioning to make a profit or is costing too much. P&Ls are often used to make big decisions to try and solve organization challenges, for example, where to invest and where to cut organization costs. However, the complexity of OE issues cannot be clearly identified at the aggregate level of an Income Statement because the tentacles of each issue weave through every aspect of the business and can't easily be seen at this level. When an Income Statement is used in this way it generally provides a short-term, short cut to reducing cost. Whilst this may be of value, or could be necessary, the lack of deeper examination may mask more complex issues and opportunities to realize hidden costs that may be of greater long-term benefit.

- Information also comes from within the organization as we continually gather data and perspectives, analyse and opine on how everything is working on the ground. We are constantly noticing, experiencing and interpreting the Behaviours of others and then evaluating and making judgements. Consequently, there is so much information flying around all the time, both formally and informally, we rarely have a chance to connect it all up or consider it thoughtfully. This creates ambiguity – all this information is open to multiple interpretations as everyone makes sense of it 'on the hoof', through their different frames of reference and from where they sit in the organization. Working out where to start your examination of the organization can feel like standing at the front of a speedboat in choppy waters, hanging on for dear life and trying to work out where you're going with spray in your eyes.

Fragmentation and surface level insight risk amplifying organization ambiguity and often make it harder for us to examine our organization and really get to the insight that will unlock OE issues.

What is the hidden cost?

When a system remains unexamined two things can happen.

- **Stagnation** – This is when an organization makes little progress towards improving OE issues. This could be because the issues are ignored, blindsided or blocked and so they never get addressed. The OE issues stay in place or get worse. Sometimes blindsiding an issue can cause circular patterns – those interminable discussions on the same topic which take considerable time and effort without making progress. At other times, organizational ambiguity prevents examination and so the deep systemic nature is never fully illuminated.
- **Expediency** – As we mentioned in Chapter 1, there is a very real pull to action in most organizations, putting pressure on us as leaders to rush to get things done. However, when we jump to deploy solutions without examining our systems, we risk skimming the surface of complex issues. Our interventions might be simplistic, focused on *either* Constructs *or* Behaviours, or solutions that include both but *ignore* the Interplay between them. The overall outcome is expediency over effectiveness – the illusion of progress.

Below are two examples to illustrate the cost of the unexamined system.

Example 1: Executive team dynamics

Scenario

An executive leadership team had been in a hybrid organization structure for some time. As they faced some complex external challenges, the hybrid structure and associated decision rights started to strain. The structure (Construct) was fostering division and fragmentation between teams which showed up in their attitude towards each other (Behaviours). This dynamic was becoming increasingly problematic (Interplay), showing up in the executive team's relationships as each member focused on protecting and supporting their own area. The CEO and CFO were reluctant to go beyond the executive team to understand issues. Instead of examining the system, a team development intervention was deployed. Over a period of 12 months, they ran three, two-day interventions, but the Interplay dynamics continued.

The costs

The visible costs are easy to spot. If we assume a conservative estimate of £10k per intervention and an executive team cost of £50k per day, this gives us a total cost of at least £330k for that year's intervention.

What isn't usually taken into consideration are the hidden costs. In this scenario there are three main areas of hidden cost:

- The Constructs around the organization structure and decision rights of the executive team were holding Behaviours in place (Interplay).
- Costs are hidden in the stagnation caused by not addressing the deeper organization issues. For example, conflict was disrupting collaboration on enterprise goals, strong silos had started to form and bed down and this also led to duplication of effort and roles, shadow functions and management time spent handling 'drama'.
- The lack of return on investment as the solution did not address the systemic nature of the issues. These issues were embedded across the whole organization, not just within the confines of the executive team.

We are not saying that team development isn't a useful intervention – it is. In this case the executive team dynamics were masking deeper organization issues. The CEO and CFO used the power in their roles to avoid a wider examination of the system. There are several possible explanations for this. They may not have fully understood how serious the problems were elsewhere in the organization or the extent of the impact on performance. They may have also been reluctant to open Pandora's box, choosing instead to contain the issue – fragmentation – by focusing on a single team. Whilst this provided a way to start somewhere – an expedient solution – it ultimately led to stagnation. A potentially powerful intervention was never given a real chance of success and, in fact, contributed to the hidden costs.

Example 2: Cost reduction

Scenario

Faced with increased operating costs, an organization needed to find £1m of savings and decided to reduce administrative support from all levels below the executive team. This resulted in the removal of 25 roles supporting sales teams. The 25 roles supported over 200 sales roles with their travel, expenses and general administration (Constructs). However, because other Constructs remained unchanged, for example, how travel was booked and expenses processed, the work stayed in place. The administrative work had to be performed by the sales roles (Behaviours). Over time, the sales teams became increasingly disgruntled and disengaged. Blame started to surface (Interplay) and this new way of working became the explanation for declining performance.

The costs

This decision made a visible saving of £1.2m, which on the surface was a good outcome. However, in reality, administrative work simply moved to more highly paid people and had the effect of reducing time with customers. Compliance issues also began to appear, with travel regularly booked outside policy and expense claims submitted incomplete or late. To tease out the hidden costs, let's assume, conservatively, that the average remuneration for a sales manager role is £150k and that 5% of time is now spent doing administration previously done elsewhere. Therefore, 5% of £150k across 200 roles is a hidden cost of at least £1.5m. So, even using our conservative estimates, this expedient solution cost more than it saved. Our cost estimate excludes the lost sales opportunities, the inevitable diversion into administrative tasks, the additional auditing required for travel expenses and the burden placed on Finance as they work to reconcile the accounts.

The executive team decided on an expedient option because they did not choose to examine the Constructs around administration. These needed to change to enable new Behaviours and fully realize the cost reduction. So, what looked like low hanging fruit was actually divisive, loaded with hidden cost and did not realize its intended outcome.

Removing administrative roles has always been a go-to cost reduction option. This choice may be even more relevant with the advent of Artificial Intelligence (AI). Many companies are starting to replace their administrative roles with AI Assistants. This could seem like an even more effective quick fix, but the fact remains that unless you have examined your system to understand the impact of such a radical change, you may still incur hidden costs you hadn't anticipated.

Summary

A thorough examination of the system leads to a deep understanding of the systemic issues, specifically the Interplays that are holding unhelpful Constructs and Behaviours in place. Fully examining your system is a precursor to unlocking hidden costs. When we ignore our receptors that are telling us something is amiss or we use power to avoid examining the system or we jump to solutions in our haste to find a way through, we make less progress than we could. We only get glimpses of the issue, and solutions look logical but don't go below the surface. This lack of examination leads to both visible and hidden costs.

Chapter 3
The cost of the status quo

'Status quo, you know, is Latin for "the mess we're in".'
Attributed to Ronald Reagan[1]

What is the status quo?

Status quo translates from Latin to mean 'the existing state of affairs'. There is something safe, predictable and familiar about the idea of the status quo for both individuals and organizations. As individuals, we experience it as our comfort zone – our familiar habits and routines that usually bring something useful or enjoyable to our lives. Organizations are similar. The status quo reflects the Interplays between lots of Constructs and Behaviours focused on particular outcomes, which become the habits and routines within the system. These interactions tend to persist, even if conditions change, because at some point in time, they provided value to the organization.

The unpredictable reality of organizations

There is, however, a catch. Our perception of the status quo as 'safe and predictable' is misleading because in reality, everything is changing all the time. Change might be sudden or imperceptibly slow, but as Heraclitus was believed to have said: 'nothing endures but change – everything flows'.[2] The only constant *is* change.

The logical implication, then, is that – both as individuals and as organizations – we would be constantly and deliberately adapting: observing, evaluating, responding and evolving our 'status quo' to attune to our surroundings. This is what happens in nature.

However, there's something in our design, as human beings, that drives us to avoid unknowns and seek safety. We crave certainty and predictability, so we behave in ways that hold familiar or favourable states of affairs in place. We do this in our own lives to maintain our comfort zone. We also do this within our organizations as we repeat familiar working patterns over and over. These are the Interplays between existing Constructs that are held in place by our Behaviours. When we get used to the way a particular Construct works in our organization, we can often feel resistance if it changes. Take reward, for example. Many of us have experienced the noise that comes with trying to implement a new reward structure, even when it is necessary for the health or survival of the business and even if the overall level of reward is comparable, with a potential for greater upside.

We live with a dilemma. The circumstances around organizations are constantly shifting, and survival depends on continual adaptation. This makes organizations inherently unpredictable. To counter this and preserve our sense of security and comfort, we tend to cling to the status quo by holding on to familiar Constructs, Behaviours and working patterns. Organization effectiveness issues arise when conditions require an organization to adapt, but instead the existing state of affairs is maintained.

The strength of the status quo

As the status quo is all about psychological security and continuity, holding onto the current state of affairs appears to protect us from having to deal with anything we might perceive as threatening. Psychologically, as human beings, we are deeply fearful of threat. Biologically, we are programmed to react to anything we perceive as a threat. It is the avoidance of this fear that underpins the strength of the status quo.

There is significant research to show that when we are threatened, our brains are hijacked by the activation of our prehistoric amygdala. This part of our brain detects threats at high speed, sending distress signals through our bodies. Our hypothalamus triggers our nervous system to release adrenaline and cortisol. This increases our heart rate and sharpens our senses; our blood sugar spikes and boosts blood flow to our muscles and brain.[3] These reactions are immediate, automatic, biological reflexes and they shape our everyday behaviour and decision-making.

The threat response theories categorize our initial reaction to threat into four automatic survival patterns, which are then shaped into a unique response, informed by awareness and choice and depending on our individual frames of reference.[4]

- **Fight** – Shows up as resistance, pushback, defensiveness, discrediting or controlling behaviour.
- **Flight** – Leads to avoidance, withdrawal or delaying decisions, deliberately ignoring or blindsiding issues.
- **Freeze** – Results in paralysis, over-thinking, swirling around issues or going blank under pressure.
- **Fawn** – Drives people to appease others, agree too readily or prioritize harmony over reality.

Fear motivates us to maintain the status quo. When we experience fear from a perceived threat our response is identical to that of personal grief. At the same time, we are seeking the fundamental human need to belong and connect and have to constantly manage the pressure of finding and holding our place in the organization hierarchy. Given we are all at the mercy of our amygdala and having to continuously navigate unpredictable systems, it's no wonder we are reluctant to step into the unknown.

Whilst we can see how the threat response shows up in individuals it may be less obvious that it also occurs at an organization level. As we covered earlier, organizations are living systems and the degree to which an organization reacts or responds dictates how successful it will be at adapting and surviving long term. Plenty of organizations have responded by clinging to their status quo – a move that ultimately contributed to their decline. Well known examples include Kodak, Blockbuster Video, Blackberry and Nokia. There are other companies who have proactively examined their external and internal environments, responded thoughtfully and adapted their status quo. Well known examples include Apple when they introduced the iPod, and Peloton who shifted from selling fitness equipment to offering a digital health and wellness platform that enables people to belong to aspirational fitness communities.

To sum up, when individuals – aggregated into systems – respond to minimize the fear of threat and hold onto what they know, they collectively reinforce the status quo. This is the strength of the living system in action. When we try to address OE issues we threaten the status quo.

Why organizations are scary

Our definition of OE clearly places accountability for OE with leaders. In practice this means we make decisions about Constructs and seek to develop ourselves and influence the Behaviours of our people, to deliver the vision and strategy of our businesses. The decisions we make continually adjust many aspects of the status quo, all the time. However, making decisions in an unpredictable environment means dealing with the reactions of others, so often driven by their fear of threat. At the same time, we have to recognize our own frames of reference including our instinctive threat responses. We are constantly navigating fear – our own and everyone else's – whether we realize it or not.

But what exactly are we all afraid of? The truth is we are not generally faced with real, life-threatening events. Our fears are often less tangible and more difficult to pinpoint. Most of the time, what we are really encountering is fear of loss and this is invariably unconscious.[5] Sometimes loss *can* be tangible, for example, losing your job or level of reward. However, even this fear can be exaggerated and can stop us adapting because of what's imagined rather than what's real. What's more prevalent, subtle and is often even more difficult to confront or engage with, is intangible, psychological loss. Examples include losing face or status, or admitting mistakes or poor judgement.

We may not name this as fear. We may experience in ourselves, and notice in others, behaviour such as resistance, reluctance, avoidance, reasoning, arguments and blame. This may show up as protecting territory or teams, avoiding giving anything up or fighting decisions that impact our roles.

So how might fear of loss actually hold the status quo in place? Below are some of the Behaviours that, at their core, are based on fear of loss.

- **Crewmates** – this is when a deep personal connection exists, for example when a leader appoints a friend into a position of power or influence and the relationship gets in the way of understanding or resolving an OE issue. The fear could be loss of connection or a loyal relationship; loss of face.

- **Anchor Weights** – This is when a leader or group has been in an organization for a long time or a part of the business has historically had significant influence and is invested in the way things are done. They become resistant to change to protect their power base or even prevent scrutiny. The fear might be loss of power, influence, status and actual roles.
- **Ink Clouds** – This is when people muddy the waters to try and avoid really examining the system. They ignore or blindside, discredit, blame and cloud the issue to prevent examination. The fear might be loss of face, role, power or even the ability to deliver particular goals they are vested in.
- **Eddies** – These are the swirls – versions of the same conversation stuck on repeat. They are commonly spotted in Constructs like governance meetings or so-called watermelon projects – the ones that appear on the surface to be on track (green) but in the depths of the project are missing key targets (red). The Behaviours that will show up will be repetitive conversations that often reopen previous discussions or decisions. The fear may be loss of credibility, loss of face, even fear of getting 'told off' by their boss.

These camouflage Behaviours hide the fear that keeps the status quo in place. There are times when we're simply unable to recognize that our own actions are getting in the way. This is why it is so important to continually develop our frames of reference and be open to influence.

What is the hidden cost?

When we protect the status quo, it generates cost. This cost is both visible and hidden. Here are some situations that may be familiar:

- **Misaligned operating models** – This is when systemic issues in how the business is set up remain unresolved. The hidden cost is wrapped up in issues like accountability gaps, conflict at senior levels leading to confusion, 'Eddies' and protracted governance.
- **Silos** – This is where separation between divisions, functions or teams remains unaddressed. This fosters a lack of cooperation and blame, leading to work getting stuck, swirling or slowing down.
- **Out of date organization design** – Instead of optimizing structures as the organization evolves, we add in roles, bolt on additional activity, ignore duplication, live with shadow functions or retain too many leadership roles.
- **Inefficient business processes** – Instead of streamlining and automating processes, we accept the way they have always been done even when they are cumbersome and serve no purpose. New people will spot pointless activities and processes immediately. There is considerable cost in maintaining out-of-date processes including the inefficiency that is absorbed in workarounds and roles.

- **Losing talent** – For example, when new people are hired to lead transformation but they hit the status quo and leave. This generates hidden costs around repeated recruitment, delays to implementation and possible reputational damage.

All of the above can lead to poor, difficult or even toxic working environments. This can also result in hidden costs due to the stress of the people in the system. It becomes visible with increased sick leave or staff turnover. The hidden costs are harder to quantify but would extend to a lack of external focus, high levels of internal politics, significant energy spent commenting on and de-coding the internal environment and widespread resistance to change.

Like the 'fish under the table' in the Fisherman's tale example, the longer complex OE issues are avoided the more they begin to smell. It's not unusual for organizations to wait years to address obvious issues with the operating model to protect individual leaders or allow legacy processes to continue even though they clearly slow the organization down. All of which create hidden costs. To look at it another way, because everything is changing all the time, areas of the business with unresolved OE issues become like swamps – they start to emit gases and cost ferments and multiplies over time. The status quo is not neutral. The longer you leave a situation that needs adapting, the more entrenched it becomes and the more difficult it is to change, as the Interplays become established and embedded. Hidden costs compound over time.

Even when you do try to address OE issues, if you rush at it without fully examining your system, you can expend a massive amount of time and energy on simplistic solutions that in the end waste resources and nothing really changes. The fish continue to smell, the swamp continues to seethe.

Confronting the reality of the status quo

Confronting, in this context, means being *willing and able* to face into the reality of the status quo to see it just as it is. We've chosen the words 'willing and able' deliberately and they are anchored in our definition of organization effectiveness covered in the Introduction.

In order to tackle complex OE issues and uncover the hidden costs, we need to be *willing* to go under the water, even step into the swamp, to discover what's really going on. We then need to be *able* to stay under, navigate and make sense of what we can now see to restore the organization to a more effective state.

- **What do we mean by 'willing'?** This is about being motivated, deciding on a course of action and remaining determined to overcome any obstacle – 'where there's a will, there's a way'. This is easily said but we all have psychological blocks that get in our way. In the case of OE issues, some of those blocks will be a threat to our autonomy, fear of failure, real or imagined conflict, limited capacity, lack of clarity or a perception that the outcome won't be worth the effort. It's as if we have our own personal tide that pulls us back. Our minds behave in similar ways to tides as they respond to forces we can't always see and can appear stubborn and unpredictable until you understand the patterns underneath. It's particularly tricky for those of us in positions of authority. Not only can we be hoodwinked by our frames of reference, to the extent that we don't see the OE issues, we can also use the power in our roles to block, avoid or sabotage others attempts to address OE issues. We all know the old adage that the higher you get the more you have to lose. It's worth remembering that the patterns that show up in our frames of reference *can* evolve because we *can* develop new and wider perspectives by being willing to step out of our personal and organizational comfort zones.

- **What do we mean by 'able'?** This is about being capable, competent and having the means (time, focus, resources and support) to step in, stay under and keep going even when faced with the strength of the system and the reaction of colleagues. Throughout the OE change journey, we need to bring people with us and leverage our work ethic – our perseverance, judgement and drive – all with serious doses of courage.

The condition that enables us to be willing and able is clarity. When we have clarity we know why it matters, what to do and where to begin. When we have clarity, our minds stop guessing, our emotional burden eases and as we begin to see the starting point, our confidence rises and uncertainty lessens. When there's a lack of clarity, even highly capable people can tread water. If goals are murky, expectations unclear, the path fragmented or the task too complex our brains interpret the situation as a threat. Clarity strengthens our capacity to be willing and able: we start to see how we can apply our skills, and have greater confidence about widening our frames of references and handling ambiguity. We are more willing to experiment and trust ourselves to figure out what's going on in the turbulent waters of the organization.

Establishing clarity, when faced with OE issues, requires an approach or methodology that can guide, equip and cut through the complexity to enable us to make sense of the reality of our organizations and work out what to do. What the rest of this book offers is a straightforward approach to examining your organization system to identify complex OE issues in a comprehensive and holistic way.

Summary

The status quo feels safe, but it is not static. In reality everything is changing all the time and when organizations do not adapt – because fear, familiarity or the strength of the system holds them in place – hidden costs accumulate and compound. The longer OE issues go unaddressed, the more entrenched the Interplays become, and the more expensive they are to unravel.

Organizations are scary places. The threat response is real – in individuals and in systems – and the Behaviours generated keep the status quo intact. The camouflage Behaviours we see in Crewmates, Anchor Weights, Ink Clouds and Eddies are not personal failings. They are the system protecting itself.

We need to be *willing and able* to confront the reality of the status quo – to see it clearly and work out a way forward.

The three chapters of Part 1 have each illuminated a dimension of why OE issues are so difficult to see and so costly to leave unexamined. Our frames of reference shape what we notice. Our reluctance to examine the system means we only ever see part of the picture. And our instinct to protect the status quo ensures that even when we do look, we may not be willing to face what's really there.

Yet, none of this is fixed. Our frames of reference can widen. Organization systems can be examined. The status quo can be confronted. Parts 2 and 3 show you how.

Part 2

The effectiveness edge

Chapter 4
An introduction to the 3D-OE Diagnostic Framework™

'A correct diagnosis is three-fourths the remedy.'
Attributed to Mahatma Gandhi[1]

Organizations are ambiguous, messy and scary environments. All this creates complexity, and complexity hides the true nature of OE issues. The unlock to OE is simple but powerful: slow down so you can speed up and start with a robust diagnostic.

The 3D-OE Diagnostic Framework™ is designed to help you 'go slow, to go fast'. Although this can feel counterintuitive and possibly indulgent in our action-oriented world, we find that slowing down, by using our diagnostic approach, gives everyone the opportunity to expand their frames of reference. This is what allows you to uncover the hidden costs of *ineffectiveness*. The methodology is also proven to surface the wisdom submerged within your organization, revealing deep insight into the systemic patterns – Constructs, Behaviours and Interplays – holding the status quo in place. With our Framework, you gain a clearer picture of what's going on before trying to solve anything and reduce the risk and cost of quick fixes that may not work.

The Framework offers a clear way for you to fully examine your organization – in part or in whole – to target the areas that require attention. It can also be used to regularly optimize performance without having to change everything. Ultimately you get at the hidden costs and improve productivity, profitability and performance.

Here are the unique attributes of the Framework:

- Is versatile and adaptable to the OE issues you face.
- Unlocks levels of organization complexity.
- Accounts for multiple frames of reference.
- Generates a 3D view – up, down and across the organization.
- Provides the structure to gather, organize and generate insights.
- Relies on genuinely listening to colleagues and respecting their perspectives.
- Designed to be inclusive.
- Encourages people to 'get their fish on the table'.

- Starts the process of winning hearts and minds.
- Mitigates the risk of expedient fixes that perpetuate stagnation.

The 3D-OE Diagnostic Framework™ is an accessible, engaging and robust way to examine your system. Using it provides clarity so you know why it matters, what to do and where to begin. When you are *willing and able*, the Framework provides insight into the hidden costs tied up in your knotty organization issues so that you can figure out how to do less of what doesn't matter and more of what does.

What is the 3D-OE Diagnostic Framework™?

The Framework is composed of a Model and a Process. Combined they unlock organization effectiveness. In this part of the book, we step through the Model and deep dive into this complex area with light hearted analogies and stories that will undoubtedly resonate with you. In Part 3 we step through the Process and the principles that underpin everything. It's worth noting that this is an integrated Framework as all the parts interact with each other to generate insight.

Explaining the Model

The Model is made up of the central OE Spine and four dynamic elements (see Figure 2).

We need to take a moment to wade through a tiny bit of theory – think of it as necessary foundations that will help you make sense of the rest of the book and equip you with the underpinning concepts. So, we're now going to take the

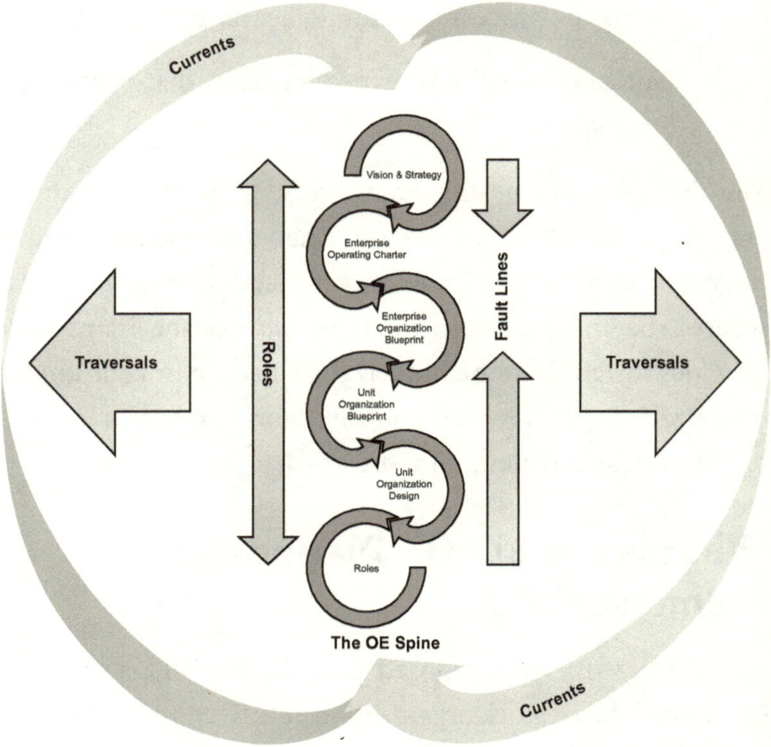

Figure 2. The 3D-OE Diagnostic Model™

Model apart, explore each element in turn, and then bring it back together.

The OE Spine

This is the centre of the Model and has to be in alignment for any organization to function optimally to deliver its vision and strategy. We use the term 'Spine' because, akin to its role in your body, it provides stability, allows movement, acts as a shock absorber and supports the communication highway between your brain and the rest of your body. When your spine is out of alignment, or worse, you damage or break it, it is painful, limiting and destabilizing. Whether we are talking about bones or business, alignment is about spotting the slipped discs or kinks in the organization system that show up as OE issues. The aim of our Diagnostic is to bring your organization back into alignment so that everything works together smoothly. Alignment of the central OE Spine is what you are striving for to unlock effectiveness in your organization.

Below is a brief explanation of each segment of the OE Spine including how each part links to the one below as depicted in Figure 3.

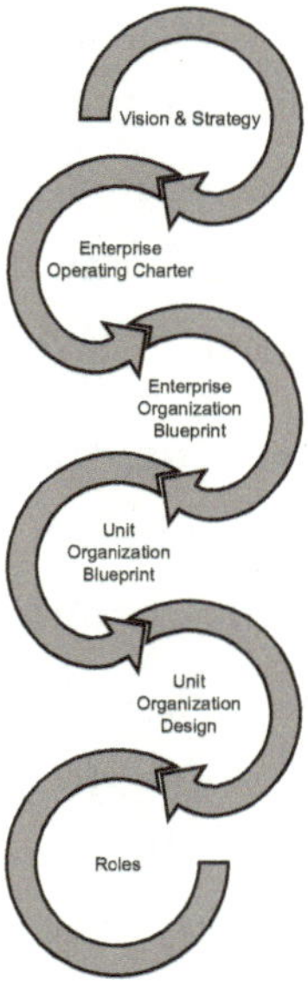

Figure 3. The OE Spine

Vision & Strategy – The Vision is the picture of the future that clarifies the direction of travel and guides decision-making. The Strategy provides the logic for how the Vision can be achieved. Strategy defines the ways in which the organization will compete – the choices that are made to pursue one approach over another. Together they provide the North Star that guides the direction of travel of the business. Without a Vision & Strategy, you have no way to keep the OE Spine in alignment.

Enterprise Operating Charter (EOC) – This is the set of agreements that outline the high-level decisions, principles and boundaries that enable the business to achieve its Vision & Strategy. It outlines how the business will deliver value to current and future customers and operate on a day-to-day basis including organization, data architecture, capabilities, processes and technology. These agreements are like a ship's log and compass combined, enabling alignment, accountability and collective behaviour.

Enterprise Organization Blueprint (EOrB) – In our Model this is a subset of the EOC and lays down clear information on how the core parts of the organization are configured and connected. What we mean by core parts are the 'buckets of work' that are required, where they are done and how they hang together. It also defines the organization principles that provide the boundaries shaping the organization's design.

Unit Organization Blueprint – This is a 'double click' on the EOrB and explains how specific areas of the organization deliver their core part of the EOrB. For example, defining a more detailed view of the buckets of work and how they are configured in a business division or functions such as finance or marketing.

Unit Organization Design – Describes how roles are organized relative to each other. This is where we get into the teams and roles depicted in organization charts. Taking finance as an example, this would be the roles organized into team structures such as accounts payable, accounts receivable and so on.

Roles – A collection of work activities with clear boundaries that one person can accomplish.

To really make sense of the way the OE Spine works, it's worth taking note of four points.

- **End-to-end alignment** – The OE Spine is not about hierarchy of leadership; it is about an aligned coherent flow of work through the organization. Sometimes leaders are tempted to use a version of the OE Spine to identify and correct OE issues. However, this approach, used in isolation, skews towards Construct alignment and doesn't address Behaviours or Interplays. We haven't found this an enduring way of dealing with OE issues.
- **Enterprise Operating Charters in practice** – You may be more familiar with calling this an Enterprise Operating Model (EOM). We use the term Charter because we deliberately want to highlight the importance of the *agreements* behind and within your business model. This is an essential point – when explicit operational agreements are made *and* implicit agreements and assumptions are surfaced *and* that's what is shared, *then* people can move together to

deliver the Vision & Strategy. Charters are not always beautifully crafted documents with a bow on them. In whatever guise a Charter shows up, it is a reflection of how the business is responding as a living organism and how it is continually adapting to deliver value and operate on a day-to-day basis. To enable alignment in the OE Spine, Charters need to have just enough detail so they are not overly bureaucratic but robust enough to provide ongoing clarity to colleagues and stakeholders. They also need to be enduring and sea-worthy, like the Ship of Theseus, so they adapt *and* hold steady as they drive multi-year investment, resource and effort.[2]

- **EOMs vs TOMs** – We've referred to the term Enterprise Operating Model (EOM). You may also use the term Target Operating Model (TOM). We commonly hear EOMs and TOMs used interchangeably and also used as a shorthand for the organization structure – these are three different concepts. It's important to note that EOMs are a description of how the business is set up *today*, whereas TOMs are future focused depicting how the business *will* be set up tomorrow. TOMs are a roadmap for change not a reflection of the current state. In the diagnostic we are focused on how the business is set up today.

- **Where concepts meet reality** – The OE Spine deliberately places emphasis on blueprinting the organization elements of the Enterprise Operating Charter. This is shown in the OE Spine at two levels – the Enterprise Organization Blueprint (EOrB) and the

Unit Organization Blueprint. It is at this point where the concept of the organization within the EOC starts to turn into reality. We commonly stay at too high a level without thinking through sufficiently how the organization needs to work on the ground, i.e. the buckets of work that are required, where it's done and how it hangs together. In this context, staying at a conceptual level seems easier because reality introduces challenges and constraints that a concept never demands that we face. All of this means we may overlook or blindside systemic OE issues.

The four dynamic elements

Below is a high-level overview that summarizes the four dynamic elements of the Model. This is to give you an overall awareness, as we'll explore each one in depth and bring to life the concepts that unlock your OE in Chapters 5–8.

The four dynamic elements build from one to the other to illuminate increasing levels of complexity.

Roles - Roles are positioned at the base of the OE Spine because Roles are the fundamental units of all organizations – like organism cells. Assuming a Role is occupied by a human being, it is the point of connection between the organization and that person. Roles bring clarity about the work needed by a person to drive value at an affordable cost. They delineate the edges within which a person has authority to operate. Individuals (and in the future the digital variety) inhabit Roles. People (and bots) shape how Roles show up through their actions and Behaviours – this is the basic Interplay in an

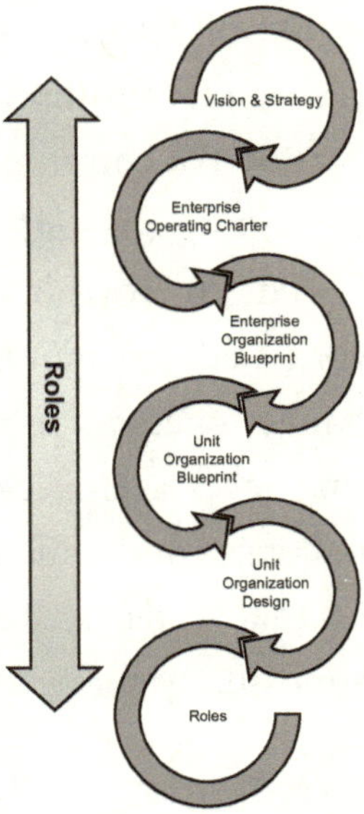

Figure 4. Roles

organization. If a Role is well positioned in an organization's structure, it would be completely aligned with all the elements of the OE Spine above it (depicted by the double ended arrow in the Model). Roles show where the work and the person or digital colleague fit into the whole system and how Roles relate to other Roles. Roles can create kinks in the OE Spine if they are misaligned (see Figure 4).

Traversals – These are the activities, areas and processes delivered by Roles that cross over organization boundaries to deliver strategic outcomes. As Traversal work moves back and forth across the system, it requires teams and Role holders to work interdependently as they reach across organization boundaries to achieve the desired result. Traversals work when there is cooperation and effective bridging mechanisms. Traversals enable cross-boundary working

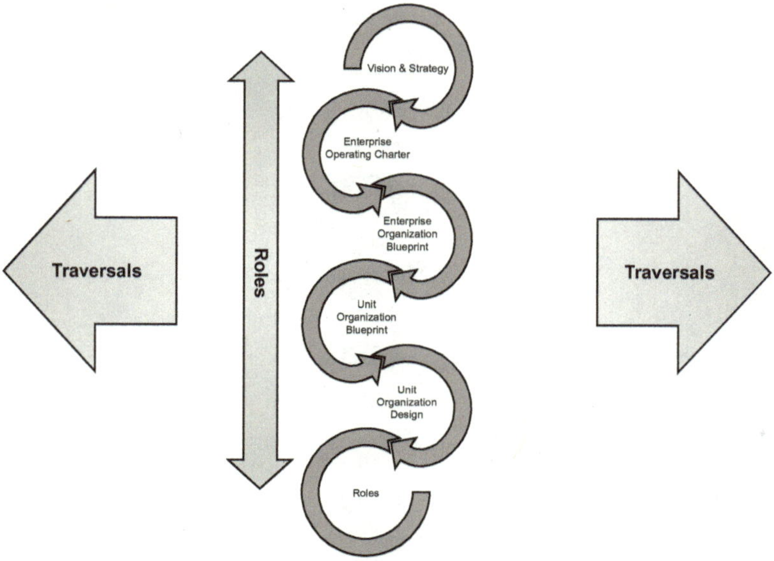

Figure 5. Traversals

and are typically located in the middle of the OE Spine, at the Enterprise and Unit Organization Blueprint levels. If Traversals are not working effectively they create issues up and down the OE Spine – with how Roles are performed and how momentum is generated to deliver the Vision & Strategy (see Figure 5).

Fault Lines – All organizations are structured in some way by boundaries and principles. Boundaries delineate the edges within the system. Some boundaries shape the organization by grouping work to ensure it is clearly distributed amongst various units and teams. Principles are ways of organizing and operating around strategic choices. Together, these boundaries and principles enable people to navigate complexity within a clear set of expectations about who is doing what and what is acceptable around here. Fault Lines occur when movement

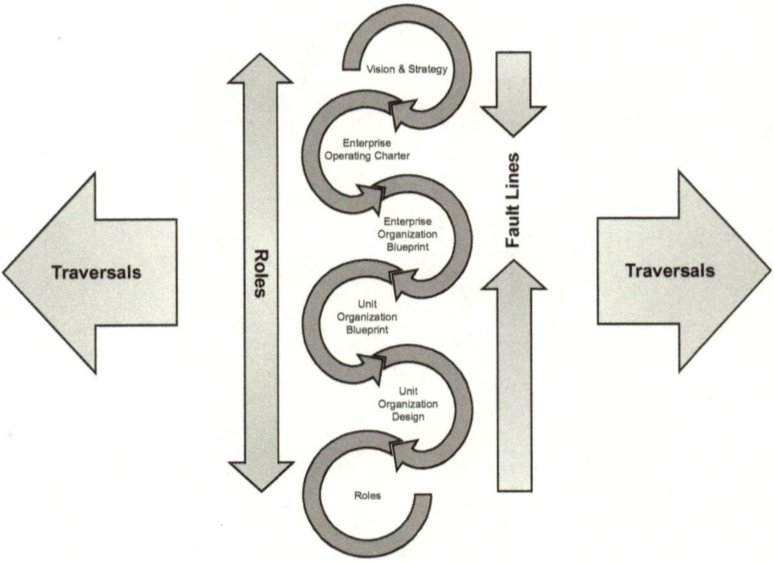

Figure 6. Fault Lines

around boundaries or principles causes fractures or misalignment in the OE Spine. When decisions or agreements are made or avoided or strategies evolve but re-alignment does not happen right down the OE Spine, Fault Lines will appear that create issues in how Roles and Traversals are performed. Fault Lines are depicted in the Model by the two opposing arrows on the right of the OE Spine (see Figure 6).

Currents - These are the accumulated patterns that have been generated from the Interplays between all the Constructs and Behaviours across the whole system. These patterns are depicted by two large arrows moving around the outside of the whole Model and connected to the top and bottom of the OE Spine. These patterns are like ocean currents – you can't always see them directly but you feel their pull. They could also be seen as the unique characteristics of the organization. Some are known because they have been around a long time and they are established. Some are more obscure and some show up in different places at different times so they are tricky and difficult to spot. Currents are all invisible forces that exert an influence on everyone and everything in the system and once discovered, they can be mapped. Some Currents will be influencing positive ways of working and valuable outcomes. However, some will be holding the organization back and can impact anywhere in the OE Spine (see Figure 7).

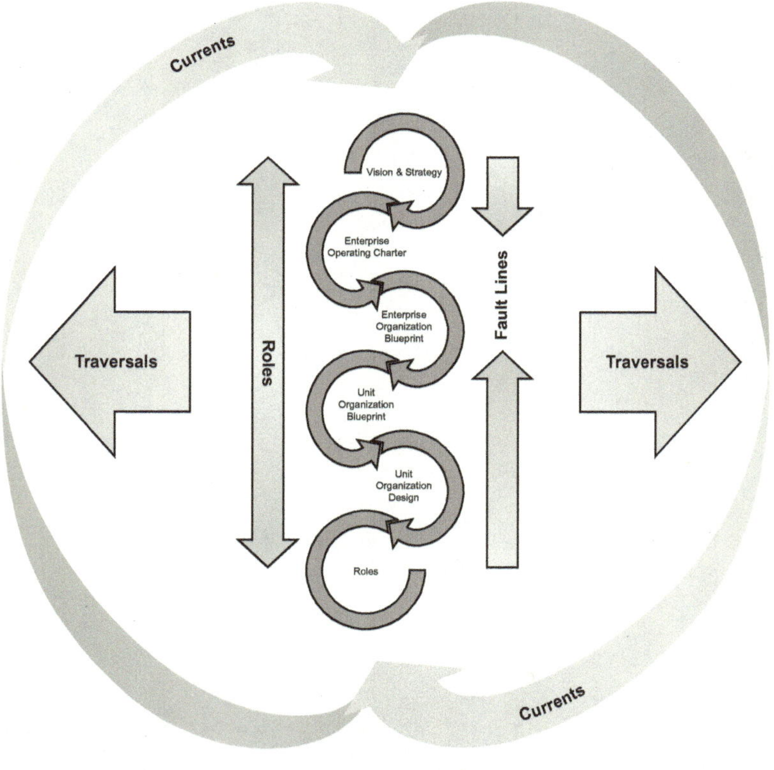

Figure 7. Currents

Summary

We need to pay attention to all four dynamic elements in the order depicted in the Model. This is because it is the best way to unravel your complex OE issues. All organizations *will have* Roles and Traversals so they need to be set up and managed to keep them working optimally all the time. All organizations will have to *live with* Fault Lines and Currents so you need to spot them, and, if they are causing issues, deal with them and mitigate their impact.

Chapter 5
Roles

The employment landscape is shifting again. Many Roles in organizations will be performed by 'digital colleagues' as Artificial Intelligence (AI) advances in sophistication. No one yet knows the eventual scale of this revolution but we have experienced transitions of this scale before and given time organizations have evolved. The need to pay attention to Roles has always been there and arguably, given the current pace of change, it is even more important. Our focus here is on Roles inhabited by people, however, so long as you have a mix of people and digital colleagues, much of what we cover is equally applicable.

What is a Role?

The Model begins with Roles because this is the simplest level of organizational complexity where OE issues consistently surface. Even though many Roles will be changed by AI in some way, they remain the basic currency of an organization.

Just as money enables the exchange of goods and services, Roles enable the exchange of work – formally through hiring and informally through everyday interactions.

Fundamentally, we need the right work done in the most productive way to achieve strategic goals. When Roles are unclear, misaligned or poorly designed, the effects ripple outward. Value leaks from the investment in people, inefficiencies take root and hidden costs accumulate, ultimately dragging on organizational effectiveness and profitability. There's also a human cost. Sub-standard Roles create psychological friction: people feel uncertain, under-used, infringed upon, overloaded or disconnected. These experiences shape not only how they feel about the organization but how well they perform within it. Many organizational problems arise from overlooking or misunderstanding how Roles function as part of the Interplay between Constructs and Behaviours.

Roles in organizations have two components: the work and the person. Interestingly, these two aspects are often conflated. We often hear leaders talking about someone's performance when, in reality, the issue relates to how the Role itself has been set up. We'll share some specific challenges that arise when leaders do this in a couple of the case studies below. Let's explore the two components.

Component 1: The work

Roles are at the base of the OE Spine. The work in a Role needs to be aligned to the strategy to mitigate against hidden costs and to create the best conditions to optimize productivity and performance. They need to meet the following six principles, in the order set out below.

To ensure Roles function effectively, they need to:

1. **Establish a point of connection with the organization** – The only way an individual can operate in any organization is through a Role which has to have some level of definition to exist.

2. **Delineate edges** – These comprise the distinct, consistent and logical set of parameters that define the boundary and content of a Role and are aligned with all the elements of the OE Spine.

3. **Scale the work to the Role** – These are constructed so that the work described in the Role can be accomplished by one person.

4. **Clarify in relation to other Roles** – Every Role functions in relation to every other Role in the system, so needs to be considered as part of this network. Some are closely linked, others are interdependent, and some are remote – yet all remain connected as part of the whole system.

5. **Give authority to act** – Roles give incumbents the authority to do work in the system.

6. **Balance value at an affordable cost** – Every Role needs to add value to the organization and be appropriately priced so there is a clear exchange of value against cost.

At a minimum, these six principles will ensure Roles are designed effectively and will give incumbents the best opportunity to perform well. When people are performing well they are more likely to be engaged and committed. It is widely accepted that stronger commitment and engagement drive greater discretionary effort.

We can bring this to life using the definition of a role in the Oxford dictionary: 'A part in a play, film or company'. It's pretty obvious in the script of a play whose part is whose. In fact, when a Director blocks a script in rehearsal you highlight the lines that constitute your part. Even though the lines are all mixed together, when highlighted, you can easily see which is your role and which is someone else's. In most productions, there are lead roles and supporting roles, which are valued differently, yet are all essential to the plot. When the play is cast, various actors read for the roles and are selected depending on their skill and suitability for the parts and their fit with the overall tone of the production. When the play is then staged everyone performs their designated role, interacting with the other roles, to create the whole show. If Romeo suddenly started speaking Juliet's lines, the production would descend into confusion and chaos. Yet scenarios like this one so often happen in our organizations.

Component 2: The person

So what happens when the two component parts of a Role – the work and a person – get together? As individuals begin to work in a Role they start to inhabit that Role, just like an actor adopts the character of their part in a play. We are not suggesting that people are deliberately pretending to be someone else. Inhabiting roles is an unconscious process that happens with all the different roles in our lives.[1] We allude to what's happening, for example, when we talk about wearing different hats. It may also explain why some people can appear one way at work and another with friends, or why they need time to decompress when moving from work to home as they transition between roles and contexts.

Roles in an organizational context are unusual because they need to be overtly defined. We have many other roles in our lives that we figure out as we're going along – parent, friend, sibling and so on. For every role we inhabit, we feel, think and interpret our experience in specific ways that show up in how we behave and relate to people who are also inhabiting their roles. In addition, every role we inhabit is situated in and influenced by a particular system or context. As soon as work and people meet through Roles in an organization, things get lively.

From the outside, all anyone can see of how another person is inhabiting a Role is 'surface level' Behaviours. If poor Behaviours show up, we usually seek to influence this by focusing on the person through performance management or coaching. Whilst these interventions are valuable and important, without also attending to the quality of the design of the Role, these steps alone may not be effective. The cost of the coaching then becomes a hidden cost as money is spent without gaining the desired outcome.

The Interplay between the work and the person

When Roles are well designed and thoughtfully positioned in the structure, there is a much better chance that the 'underwater' elements (feeling, thinking and sense-making) are positive and therefore are more likely to generate constructive Behaviours. If Roles are set up poorly, this could contribute to individuals feeling, thinking and interpreting their experiences more negatively as they wrestle with the impact of issues within their remit. This can certainly impact individual performance. Depending on the size and importance of the Role, like a ripple effect, it could also cause real damage to the effectiveness of the organization.

Conversely, not only do Roles leave their mark on us, we leave ours on them. When individuals inhabit Roles they shape how a Role shows up – over time, their Behaviours can change the Role itself. As soon as someone steps into a Role it evolves as they bring their talents, experiences and way of working. When someone else takes it on, it becomes something different again.

An individual and an organization are fundamentally linked through a Role (see Figure 8).

Roles also morph as organizations develop their capabilities including technology advances. They can become more important, change size and scope or become outdated as the direction and needs of the organization change or because of external influences. If you create or change something in one Role, it could have unintended consequences in another.

Roles are pivotal Constructs in organizations. Despite this, designing and structuring Roles well is a neglected area. The reality is that in the hurly burly of organization life, most of us take Roles more or less on trust. We might spend time

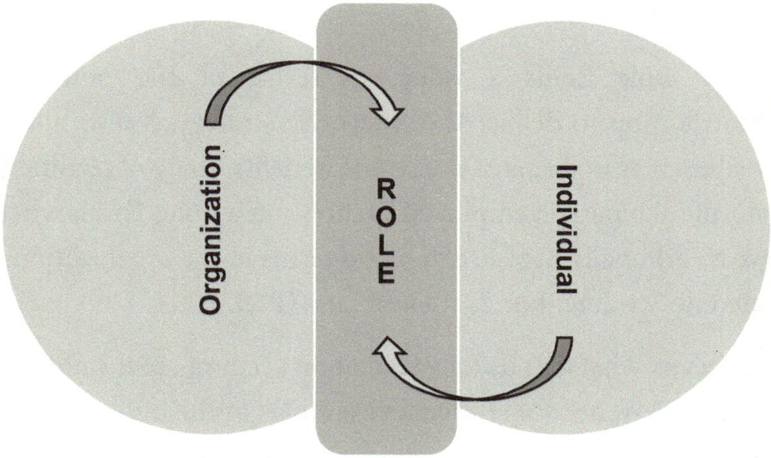

Figure 8. Role model

writing a profile if we want to recruit someone, but for the most part, everyone is simply too busy getting on with the ever-changing day job to spend any time thinking about Roles. To add to the yawn factor, the recruitment process can be cumbersome and usually requires you to fill in a job description with all sorts of unnecessary fields. You just need a warm body, as quickly as possible, to be able to cover all the workload.

If there was more focus on Roles, fewer OE issues would arise, and greater organization performance could result. Roles come up throughout a Diagnostic as they show up in the different levels of organization complexity.

The value at stake

We diminish Roles by looking at them through our existing frames of reference, not examining them in relation to the system and perpetuating the status quo. This hides cost.

Commercial cost

Every Role holds a value, in terms of the potential contribution to deliver the enterprise strategy. It also holds visible costs in terms of the salary, benefits, share of facilities, etc. of each person employed to carry out a Role. This is what we traditionally measure in broad terms in the organization's Income Statement or Profit and Loss (P&L).

However, what isn't usually taken into account are the hidden costs. Below are some specific examples of the hidden costs, which we've organized around the six Role principles. In reality, if there are problems with a Role, it's likely that more than one of the principles will not have been applied.

- **Establish a point of connection with the organization.** Sometimes Roles disappear altogether and individuals or even whole teams are left floating, not adding value but still in the system.

  Example: Consultants were brought in and they took over the remit of internal subject matter experts (SMEs). This left the internal incumbents disenfranchised and disaffected and in essence doubled the cost to the organization.

- **Poorly delineated edges.** When the parameters and content of a Role are poorly designed this may lead to: mismatched hires, the cost of repeating a recruitment process, the lost productivity of a person performing in a way that's at odds with what's actually needed and vacant Roles. We've often seen talented people recruited into Roles that look clear on paper but prove to be misaligned or overlapping with other Roles once the individual joins the business.

Example: One company hired an expensive Marketing Director using a poorly delineated Role. It sounded great when described during the recruitment process, but once in the system the new incumbent was pulled in multiple directions as she realized the Role she had been sold wasn't at all clear. She found herself in many tricky situations as she tried to interpret and act into the Role as she understood it when other colleagues had very different interpretations of what the Role edges were.

- **Work is scaled to be too big or too small for one person.** Whether the Role is too big or too small, the result can often be patchy productivity, loss of talent and repeated recruitment costs.

  Example: Multiple new accountabilities were added to an existing Role over time. They were not accompanied by any related uplift in recognition and remuneration and eventually the Role became too big for the Role holder to accomplish and slowly generated a sense of discontent.

- **Unclear in relation to other Roles.** Here, Roles or functions may overlap or leave gaps in how work is done. This usually generates confusion, competitiveness, complexity, swirling and delays productivity as people circle around working out who is accountable for what. Work gets duplicated and multiple meetings spring up, often full of expensive people. This often happens when centralized shared services or centres of expertise are created or when activities move to digital colleagues.

Example: A shared services function was implemented in an organization, and some new Roles were added without aligning them with existing ones. The original teams still continued to do the same work, which ran in parallel, generating hidden cost.

- **A Role is not given the right level of authority to act.** At other times, Roles are clearly designed but are not positioned well enough – this may be across organization boundaries or within the team. This can lead to personal frustration for Role holders, can hamper individual productivity and lead to talent leaving. Roles positioned at too low a level in the hierarchy for the incumbent to have sufficient influence over more senior stakeholders will impact pace and limit productivity. On the other hand, Roles positioned at too high a level in the structure, to try and attract talent for example, can result in quick turnover because the recruit is too big for the actual level of authority in the Role.

  Example: An individual is hired as a Managing Director (MD) for a local market. On arrival they realize they don't have full accountability for the country P&L because of the extent of the remit of the centralized functions. For example, Manufacturing had accountability for the cost of goods. In this instance the positioning of the Role as an MD gave a false impression of the authority of the Role.

- **Value isn't balanced against an affordable cost.** These might be Roles that are now out of date as the Vision & Strategy has changed but they are continuing to deliver legacy goals. They could be Roles shaped around an individual's agenda or Roles aligned to poorly defined change programmes. There could also be instances where they are inhabited by individuals who are occupying a Role that is beyond their capability. The cost could be hidden in extra or misaligned Roles, unnecessary activity, outdated ways of working and slower delivery.

  Example: A review revealed that several additional Roles had been added to a team to compensate for the poor performance of the team leader. Parts of his accountabilities had been distributed within his team. Once performance had been addressed and the team had been properly designed, three Roles were removed. The remaining colleagues were clear about their Role edges and the cost of the team was reduced.

All of these issues generate visible and hidden costs and can impact performance. They also show up as friction in the system such as political fights, dissent and drama which also impact people in a negative way. Role issues often mask deeper systemic issues in the OE Spine.

Cost to individuals

Roles that are unclear, poorly positioned, have morphed unchecked over time or have been impacted by organization changes tend to generate confusion in the individuals inhabiting those Roles. The impact is at a psychological, 'underwater' level and is often difficult to see and may build up slowly over time. The impact on self esteem, no matter the seniority of the person, shouldn't be underestimated. Inhabiting a substandard Role can go deep and leave scars. What we see on the surface might be conflict and changes in Behaviours, for example frustration, anger, resistance or withdrawal. There may also be a drop in performance, either suddenly or incrementally. However, below the surface all manner of stress and crises could be happening as individuals battle with the hidden psychological cost of faulty Roles. There may be visible costs to the organization which can be measured in terms of the number of people being signed off for mental health reasons or leaving altogether. There are also costs hidden in the time spent by individuals trying to make sense of their situation and management time seeking to resolve issues.

Understanding issues with Roles

The first thing we look for when we start to analyse diagnostic data is issues with Roles. We've found that by starting with Roles, other more complex problems start to reveal themselves – themes and patterns that thread through Role issues. Roles are like the sediment at the bottom of the ocean – there is so much rich information that can tell you about the history, variety and health of everything that's lived or lives in that environment.

Below are a few case studies that have been synthesized from many different companies to illustrate how issues with Roles can show up and the hidden costs in terms of lost opportunity. We've also outlined the Role issues that are likely to emerge with the advancement of AI in organizations. The case studies are not meant to be exhaustive but illustrate some typical ways in which problems with Roles arise – or may arise in the future.

Case study 1: Confusing the two components of a Role – work and person

Context

A company decided to radically shift its strategic direction and so required new capability to develop the strategy and evolve the business model. Two new Roles were created in different functions of the business both of which were focusing on the organization-wide business model. As the two individuals began working in their respective Roles, it became clear that something was amiss.

Scenario

As issues around the work began to emerge and progress on the business model stalled, their respective bosses assumed the challenges were about individual performance. They only looked at the presenting Behaviours, rather than how the Roles might be generating these Behaviours.

How the issue showed up

Both individuals were working hard to perform their accountabilities. They complained about each other and experienced the other as either stepping into their domain or not picking up accountabilities they thought the other should be owning. Both individuals had been extremely successful before joining the organization. Both individuals reacted differently with one person withdrawing and the other shifting direction completely to try and find their own space.

When each Role was analysed, the functional leaders realized the Role designs were ambiguous and open to interpretation as the edges of each Role were unclear. It was also apparent that both Roles had been designed in isolation with no reference to how each one related to the other. As soon as the Roles were clarified, the individuals began to work together well, with each one operating within the same domain, but delivering different, complementary aspects of the goal.

Estimated cost to the organization

Two senior Roles are out of kilter.

- Estimated fully loaded cost of senior leaders: £400k
- Individual hourly rate based on a 7-hour working day: £220
- Estimated duration of the issue: 9 months (39 weeks)
- Estimated weekly time spent on unproductive activity due to the issue: 5 hours per week
- Estimated total cost = 2 Roles × £220 × 39 weeks × 5 hours = £85,800

By allowing this situation to continue hidden costs result, as outcomes are delayed, frustrations have a ripple effect on other Roles and individuals spend time on 'Eddies' – i.e. swirling and repetitive activity that is not contributing to the Vision & Strategy. Think of this as the equivalent cost of one experienced manager Role being funded per annum.

In summary, when the design of a Role is out of kilter, it can be surprisingly hard to see what's really going on. We often jump to conclusions about the individual in the Role. That's not to say people and teams never underperform – but it's always worth establishing first whether the issue is with the Role before assuming it's about the person. Watch for good people going off peak performance, new friction in the system or shifts in Behaviours such as withdrawal or anger.

Case study 2: Designing around people

It's common for leaders to conflate the Role and the person – here we have two scenarios to illustrate this challenge.

Scenario one

In a reorganization focused on greater efficiency and a reduction in costs, a leader presented their organization chart with only the names of people, not the Role titles.

How the issue showed up

The leader was unable to objectively think about an effective organization design because they were seeing people not Roles. Consequently, they struggled to take Roles out of their structure or to change the boundaries or content of Roles. They could only see the 'good people' in the Roles, not the Roles themselves.

The hidden cost is buried in the leader's inability to adjust the status quo of their team and the ensuing stagnation as their structure stayed the same and they failed to identify a reduction in costs or opportunities for efficiency.

Scenario two

Work was placed in a Role because the leader favoured an individual (Crewmates). The type of work was more aligned with other Roles in his team.

How the issue showed up

Friction showed up in the team as peers with more expertise in the work tried to support the favoured person. This individual was ill-equipped to do the work.

Estimated cost to the organization

Three managers support a fourth manager who does not have the appropriate expertise for the work.

- Estimated fully loaded cost for each manager: £200k
- Hourly rate for each manager based on a 7-hour working day: £110
- Estimated duration of the issue: 18 months (78 weeks)
- Estimated weekly time spent on unproductive activity due to the issue: 3 hours per person per week
- Estimated total cost = 3 managers × £110 × 78 weeks × 3 hours = £77,220

As the team was dependent on the outputs of this individual, which were sub-standard, this diminished the overall value the team was able to contribute to the business. This is a hidden cost.

These scenarios are hardly surprising given people inhabit Roles. The Role and the person become one, just like an actor in a play. You know the actor you're watching isn't really the character they are portraying, but we suspend reality so we can enjoy the illusion of the show. The same thing happens in organizations. We are unconsciously taken in by the illusion that the person and the Role are one and the same. They are not. Whilst there is an intrinsic link between a Role and the person inhabiting the Role, we need to be able to separate them and see them distinctly.

Case study 3: Positioning cross-functional Roles

Context

A company needed to inject more energy and resources into the end-to-end automation of back-office systems to better serve their customers as well as to boost growth. They introduced a new Role designed to facilitate this journey and act as a bridge across multiple functions to facilitate the smooth implementation of the new system and ways of working.

Scenario

As the Role expanded over time, it was positioned in the system as a Director of Operations. The intent was to provide the Role with the authority to act to ensure adoption of the new systems including the smooth and speedy identification and embedding of new processes as various functions got involved. However, the necessary range of Constructs, such as level in the organization, reward systems and team structure, that would have given the Role holder authority, weren't put in place.

How the issues showed up

The Role title was misleading, creating confusion leading to blame (Ink Clouds). People were using the title as a proxy for either explaining or decoding the scope, influence and positioning of the Role. The Role was still principally about facilitation to surface critical issues, broker alignment across teams and guide them on the path to timely resolution rather than being accountable for running operations. Yet the 'Director of Operations' title inferred greater decision-making authority that was not recognized in other functions. The situation was exacerbated because the level of authority of these Roles had not been well communicated and embedded across the business.

The confusion showed up in slow and inconsistent decision-making leading to multiple meetings and swirling around issues.

Estimated cost to the organization

Director of Operations has one extra meeting per week for 2 hours with each representative from five impacted functions to try and make progress or decisions.

- Estimated Director of Operations fully loaded cost: £500k
- Hourly rate based on a 7-hour working day: £275
- Estimated fully loaded cost of functional representatives: £200k
- Hourly rate: £110
- Estimated duration of the issue: 6 months of unproductive meetings (26 weeks)

- Estimated total cost = (2 hours × £275 × 26 weeks) £14,300 + (2 hours × 5 people × £110 × 26 weeks) £28,600 = Total £42,900

The hidden cost is again located in lost opportunity as implementing the new system is slower and people's time is tied up in unproductive activity and Behaviours. This cost outlined above only takes into account one extra weekly meeting. It's likely there were many more meetings and informal discussions on this issue and again the magnitude of lost opportunity starts to come into focus.

Roles that are intended to operate across functional boundaries, whether the organization model is formally matrixed or not, are particularly tricky and need careful design, positioning and embedding. Only then can incumbents be properly set up for success.

Case study 4: Lack of alignment around the Role of teams or functions

The case studies so far have all focused on individual Roles. Issues can also arise with lack of clarity around the Role of a team or function.

Scenario

A regulatory function had strong links to the external regulatory bodies and embedded ways of working. The products carried a high level of risk in a highly regulated sector. However, in this scenario the regulatory function was increasingly being perceived by the commercial teams as blockers to the innovation of new products into the market.

How the issue showed up

The regulatory team saw themselves as trying to support the business by raising legitimate challenges as new products were developed. The commercial functions experienced the regulatory team as always saying no, often at a late stage in product development. Where the two functions were at odds, was around their frames of reference about the Role of the regulatory function. The way the leader of Regulatory interpreted the Role of the function inevitably shaped the design of every Role in the team and therefore influenced the Behaviours of how the team showed up.

The regulatory team believed their Role was principally to protect the organization and ensure it was complying to external regulatory requirements. Whilst this is indeed a legitimate and crucial Role of the function, the way in which this was being executed had become too literal and rigid to fully support the pace of growth.

> The commercial function needed the regulatory team to keep them safe and play a more enabling Role by supporting them to navigate the external regulations with a certain amount of considered risk. They needed the team to continue to challenge *and* act as a guide and coach, shifting away from purely policing.

The cost hidden in the lost revenue from a delayed or missed market proposition would be significant; inevitably there would be multiple meetings needed to unblock issues; missed deadlines would cause a knock-on impact on resourcing, planning and work throughout the organization and finally a potential impact on reputation in the marketplace. There is also the human cost of the frustration and finger pointing from both sides that impacted the working environment. Multiply these by whole teams or functions and the scale of the hidden cost is material.

The future of roles

The AI revolution is underway and will undoubtedly bring huge benefits to the bottom line and the efficiency of organizations. It will reshape roles, initially by taking over routine, rules-based tasks, requiring humans to monitor and oversee AI outputs and make complex judgements. New job categories will emerge that are focused on optimizing AI, some roles will disappear and many existing roles will need to be reconfigured as they are augmented by AI.

One of the most significant impacts will be on the role of the leader. Strategically we will have to understand how AI will enhance our business and figure out what changes we will need to make along the OE Spine. On a day-to-day basis we need to pay attention to the specific configuration of work between humans and AI agents. As an example, we are starting to get familiar with automated tasks being done by AI 'digital assistants', but AI agents go one step further, they become 'digital colleagues'. AI agents are autonomous systems with the power to assign tasks, track performance and make decisions – functions once reserved for humans. AI agents are starting to handle the responsibilities once owned by supervisors, team leaders and even directors. So, at some point we are going to be supervising AI agents who are supervising our people. The organizations that will be effective will be those that *intentionally* design all Roles, including those inhabited by digital colleagues.

The impact of AI roles in organizations is yet to be fully understood. Some of the risks we foresee could be: the emergence of shadow activity if the use of AI becomes a shortcut to cross boundary collaboration; AI is implemented in a piecemeal way or as an IT project without due consideration to other roles in the enterprise; if gaps emerge between the activities carried out by AI and those done by humans.

Our hypothesis would be that to successfully realize the advantages, we will need an even deeper understanding of how our organization functions and how work flows through AI and non-AI Roles. Simply put, if we don't really understand the work, and how the work is apportioned into Roles, whether it is done by humans or bots it is not going to be effective. At the end of the day, it will still be vital that a human somewhere is accountable for the quality and integrity of the output.

A focus on Roles will continue to be vital, even though the nature of Roles and who does them is going to change. The six Role principles will still apply.

Summary

We can't emphasize enough the importance of Roles. Roles are positioned at the base of the OE Spine of the 3D-OE Model because they are the fundamental units of all organizations. They are the pivotal connection between an organization and the role holder. A Role is the basic Construct that enables work to flow up, down and across the system and creates the conditions in which a person can flourish. As we said earlier the work in a Role needs to be aligned to the Vision & Strategy to mitigate against hidden costs and to create the best conditions to optimize productivity and performance.

It's worth noting just how much leverage every leader has at their disposal to create the best conditions for their people to perform, simply by paying attention to Roles. When leaders do the work to design, position and embed Roles that are aligned to the Vision & Strategy, and organize them into sensible structures, they go a long way to preventing issues with Roles arising. This would significantly reduce hidden costs and impact the bottom line.

Chapter 6
Traversals

We define Traversals as those Constructs that enable cross-boundary working which is essential in any organization. This moves us to the next level of complexity when diagnosing OE issues. We start to look at how Roles fit into the organization system, specifically in relation to work that needs to flow across boundaries. We are therefore looking beyond individual functions and units, at the Blueprint level of the OE Spine. We will start looking at aspects that you will perceive intuitively, will have undoubtedly wrestled with in your mind but may not have seen these explicitly codified in the way we are going to cover them here.

Cross-boundary working is about joining up work to enable it to ebb and flow across the organization. All organizations have virtual, physical, informal and formal boundaries. Obvious boundaries might be a floor, site or building that creates a literal, physical boundary. We also hold boundaries in our minds. If you think about the name of a function, you're likely to draw an invisible line around groups of people doing certain types of work. Organization structures also introduce both formal and informal boundaries: the neat boxes of an organization chart on the one hand, and the lived, often messier experience, of how people actually interact on the other. Whether an organization's design is hierarchical, matrixed or a hybrid, boundaries are always present and always shaping Behaviours. It's worth noting that any system, process or function that operates in isolation invokes a boundary that needs to be noticed.

To help make sense of this we are going to break down the concept of Traversals into its constituent parts, then bring it back together to look at it from an organization system perspective.

What is traversing and what are Traversals?

Work needs to move across the various organizational boundaries. This needs to be actively facilitated by Constructs and Behaviours. In this context we call the Constructs 'Traversals' and the Behaviours 'traversing'. We will explore the Behaviours first as it helps to make sense of the Construct.

Traversing

Traversing means to move back and forth, sideways, across, through or over something, typically in a deliberate or purposeful way. As a term it's often used to describe covering ground, navigating difficult terrain or crossing a space – whether physical, metaphorical, virtual or invisible. Going back to our marine analogy, whether for survival, ambition or enlightenment, ever since the days of Magellan and Columbus, traversing the ocean has been viewed as a profound act that is noted as courageous and continues to inspire awe and amazement.

In the ocean, many species traverse vast distances in search of food, shelter or mates. However, typically the octopus stays within a defined home range, rarely travelling any distance at all. Octopuses are independent, self-reliant and autonomous, navigating alone and relying on their intelligence, adaptability and camouflage to survive.

In an organization context, every person needs to forge their own path, choosing their next step on a moment-by-moment basis depending on their surroundings. Sometimes people will be in the open, and at other times use camouflage or other tactics to keep going. Like the octopus, individuals traverse the organization independently in order to survive and thrive. It is essential that people can take care of themselves, navigate obstacles and deal with predators. Organizations are unpredictable environments just like the ocean.

As part of their role, everyone has to traverse across an organization. However, every organization has roles that require more sophisticated traversing Behaviours, for example, people in business partnering roles in a matrix set-up, medical affairs in a pharmaceutical company or roles in a risk function in financial services. This is because the work these roles do is dependent on cross boundary working.

Sophisticated traversing requires people to not only operate within their defined home range like the octopus, and remain independent but also exercise *INTERdependence.* Unlike independence, which emphasizes self sufficiency, interdependence requires substantive connections, mutual reliance and the judicious exercise of power. In human relationships, interdependence fosters cooperation, alliances and support. Recent research reveals that certain patterns of behaviour impact the depth and breadth of connections a person can develop. These are: the number of people they are connected to and the degree of influence these connections have, how they control information across boundaries – whether they build bridges or create walls and the ability to build alliances based on trust.[1] These patterns of behaviour describe what we mean by interdependence and are essential for sophisticated traversing in an organization. One additional nuance is that in organizations traversing is not about hierarchy but about catalyzing action from anyone who touches cross-boundary work whether they are the CEO or an entry level role. Any of these people can exercise their power to block the flow of work as it moves across the system.

The reason it's important to understand the nature of how people traverse organizations is because Traversals, which we explore next, require these very specific Behaviours to work effectively.

Traversals

Traversals are organizational Constructs that enable people in their roles to work across boundaries and drive the strategic outcomes at the top of the OE Spine. To varying extents every role in an organization has to work across boundaries, so the focus here is on the roles that require more sophisticated Behaviours – traversing. Traversals focus on roles that include activities and/or are situated in an area that sits between other functions and/or contributes to core processes. If any role has activities, areas or processes that require working across boundaries, then there is a dependency on people inhabiting those roles in such a way that they actively traverse across boundaries, as described above. If they cooperate effectively the Traversal Construct is optimized through their Behaviours. If activities, areas or processes start to get stuck or noisy it will be an indication that people are not traversing and cooperating well enough.

We have identified three types of Traversal to enable the diagnosis of OE issues. All three Traversals are held in roles to some degree. The role is pivotal (see Figure 9).

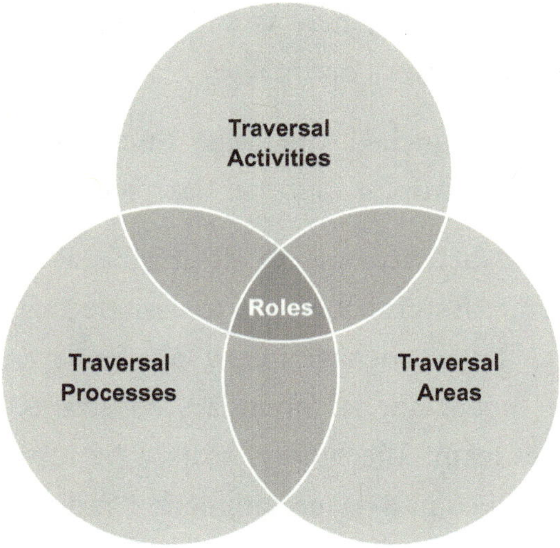

Figure 9. Traversals

Below are some examples where we have focused only on one type to illustrate what they are and why they have a material cost to the organization. It is important to note that the three types of Traversals rarely show up in isolation as they are interconnected with each other.

Traversal activities – All activities directly or indirectly connect across an organization. However, there are some activities that have greater significance because they have multiple touchpoints *and* are key to delivering the organization's strategic outcomes. These are the activities where the role or team has to act at the centre of a network and pull on expertise elsewhere in the organization. It's these Traversal activities that we are interested in. Examples include innovation in med tech, insights in fast moving consumer goods (FMCG) organizations or actuarial activity in the insurance industry.

To illustrate the point, here is an example of a Traversal activity that didn't work optimally.

- Clairol launched the 'Mist Stick' curling iron – however, 'Mist' in German slang means 'manure'.

The Traversal activity was to determine a local market product name. It's probably safe to assume that the global brand team did not behave interdependently and traverse across the organizational boundary to connect with the local market team. The hidden costs were lost revenue as the product failed in the German market and the significant expense and effort required to withdraw and rebrand the product.

Traversal areas – These are specialist areas that sit between two or more parts of the business. They operate as bridging units between key functions. In the charity sector, for example, it may be a fundraising team that sits between marketing and finance. In consumer goods businesses, it might be channel marketing that sits between sales and marketing. Another example is payroll that sits between HR and finance.

The problem with Traversal areas is that they have to be 'homed' somewhere but arguably they never truly fit anywhere because their work crosses organization boundaries. Traversal areas have to rely on the people within them cooperating interdependently. If the people are not cooperating, what often happens is leaders leap to the conclusion that it's the location of the area that's wrong. This shows up as perennial discussions (Eddies) or the periodic changing of reporting lines from one area of the business to the other, without solving the issue.

Here are a few examples of problematic Traversal areas where the focus remained on where it should be homed (the Construct) rather than people cooperating with each other (the Behaviours):

- A channel marketing team that produced collateral which brand marketing loved but was viewed as unusable by the sales teams. This led to a regular discussion about moving the team to sales.

- A marketing team that purchased agile digital technology that didn't work with the company's legacy systems. This led to the decision to move digital marketing to IT. In this case as soon as it was moved to IT, the discussion then became about moving it to marketing.
- A payroll function that reported to HR due to confidentiality and data privacy concerns but was isolated from the finance month-end processes. This led to perennial discussions on whether the payroll team should be part of HR or finance.
- A procurement function that reported to finance to drive cost reductions. Due to a lack of cooperation with the supply chain team and difficulties with raw material shortages, there were repeated discussions about whether the reporting line should be changed.

Traversal processes - As with activities, all processes connect across an organization to some extent, even if it's only a handoff to another function or team. There are some processes, however, that are more significant than others because they drive the core work of the business. They are all, in some way, central to the delivery of the organization's Vision & Strategy. One example is cash flow in the building industry, often called order-to-cash in other sectors. This process is core to revenue generation, cash flow and customer satisfaction. Another is procure-to-pay which covers everything from identifying and contracting suppliers through to issuing payments and is essential for controlling spend, optimizing working capital and having the right suppliers available when needed. We could also consider all the processes related to the employment of people, so called 'cradle to grave', as a core process. Yet despite the centrality and significance of such Traversal processes, they are often hampered by boundary issues that stifle alignment and co-operation and instead generate significant but invisible costs.

How do Traversals show up in the organization system?

If you have work that has to move across organization boundaries to fulfil the Vision & Strategy, then you have a Traversal. Traversals are like Russian dolls – they have multiple elements nested inside each other. The Constructs and Behaviours include:

- All the activities, areas and processes within that Traversal.
- How those activities, areas and processes show up in Roles.
- How those Roles connect with each other to ensure the work flows across organization boundaries.
- How the people inhabiting the Roles behave to traverse in a sophisticated way to make the Traversal work.

When things go wrong, get a bit noisy or get stuck something in that Traversal is not set up properly. It's either the Constructs, the Behaviours or a combination of both, so that the Interplay between them needs to be examined.

Eco-systems

There are some specific disciplines and areas of expertise that are increasingly hard to operate as Traversals particularly in large organizations. Common examples include data, data privacy, insights, strategy and digital. This is because they can't be homed in a single area or solved by processes alone. These disciplines need to exist as an eco-system. Eco-systems look simple on the surface but are in fact an intricate network of dynamic relationships. We need to recognize that, in an organizational ecosystem, different parts of the business will inevitably coexist and will have to actively connect. Deliberately designed Constructs (e.g. roles, processes, etc.) that support and shape the essential cooperative Behaviours are even more vital as these areas are breeding grounds for duplication, overlap and hidden cost.

The outcome we're aiming for is that people can actively rely on each other across an ecosystem's boundaries, even while working in different areas of the business. Issues with eco-systems have to be examined as a network, looking across the whole system.

Understanding issues with Traversals

Before we share some case studies, it's worth further understanding why Traversals break down.

As noted above, all organizations come with virtual, physical, informal and formal boundaries. When these boundaries go awry, fragmentation occurs. In organization parlance, we commonly refer to the separation that forms as 'silos'. Organizational silos are parts of a business – regions, divisions, business units, functions, teams – that operate in isolation rather than as connected parts of a whole. They tend to develop their own priorities, rhythms and loyalties, more often than not at the expense of wider organizational effectiveness. Silos show up in *all* organizations. So much so, that silos could be seen as a naturally occurring phenomenon of any Construct with people in it. As humans we are programmed to form communities or tribes with people who are like us – back to the unpredictability and security dilemma covered in Chapter 3. We do this to feed our need to belong to a group. The trouble starts when silos become rigid, which gets in the way of people traversing across organization boundaries.

We explored under 'Traversing' (above) how critical *interdependent* Behaviours are to make Traversals work. Despite extensive thought leadership on roles like business partnering, issues with Traversals are still commonplace. One hypothesis about why Traversal issues remain so prevalent could be due to the limitation of all humans on the number of relationships we can sustain. This has been explored in documented research and notably the bestselling book 'The Social Brain', in which the Dunbar Graph summarizes the typical sizes of layers in personal social networks and therefore corresponding psychological closeness.[2] The book is well worth a read, but in the meantime here are two interesting findings that illustrate why rigid silos are so prevalent in organizations.

1. **'The Dunbar number'** – The authors found that 150 is the limit on the number of people we are willing to act altruistically towards on the basis of personal knowledge and out of a sense of obligation.

People inhabit roles and roles are pivotal to well functioning Traversals, where people cooperate across boundaries. However, in large complex organizations the 150 limit could be exceeded in the person's home function before they even start to cross organization boundaries. We've also pondered if, in this increasingly social media-driven society, the 150 limit is regularly exceeded by our participation in virtual online communities and if that spills over into the work setting.

2. **'60% of our social effort is devoted to just 15 people'** – Their research supports what we experience day-to-day in most organizations – that we have strong bonds with small clusters of people which reinforces internal cohesion, but this potentially limits cross-group collaboration. In other words when individuals feel a strong sense of belonging within their immediate circle, they are less likely to seek interactions beyond it, unintentionally strengthening barriers and gaps between groups. Whilst this can be beneficial for cohesion within a team, it is problematic for broader cooperation between teams. Additionally, the fear of losing that sense of belonging can make individuals hesitant to challenge group norms or advocate for integration with outsiders.

Whilst silos may be a 'fact of life', when they harden, they impact the performance of the organization, getting in the way of driving towards common outcomes.

Sub-optimal Traversals generally become visible through Behaviours, for example when the Behaviours we describe in Chapter 3, such as Ink Clouds and Eddies, are evident. Here are some examples of how issues with Traversals show up:

- Individuals 'over belonging' to particular leaders, teams or functions. This is often prevalent in the early stages of mergers and acquisitions, as people stay where they feel safe. If the merger or acquisition is badly handled the resulting organization trauma just further embeds the silos as the boundaries become excessively rigid *and* people identify too strongly with their home side.

- A pattern where a leader requires that information, work and decisions go up the hierarchy to them before being allowed to cross over to another team or when a leader requires information to come to them first before being disseminated down the hierarchy for action. The hierarchical Behaviours of these leaders will create rigid silos that get in the way of a more natural flow of information that would usually travel in many directions.

- Matrix structures that were introduced with the motivation to save cost rather than to truly facilitate cross-boundary working. Often in these instances formal connectivity occurs only at the top of the organization, so it adds more confusion and creates silos further down. What we tend to hear in problematic matrix structures are leaders that are spoken about as being 'loyal to one camp', teams that don't serve both masters, end-to-end processes that have problematic gaps or functions/divisions that are spoken of as 'fortresses'.

In all of the examples above, the presence of the rigid silo can be the result of issues with either Constructs or Behaviours which then generate the Interplay that holds them in place. From a hidden cost perspective the rigid silo fragments the external and internal customer experience, prevents a focus on the bigger picture, creates mistrust, slows down innovation, stops us learning from past mistakes and creates duplication.

It's worth noting that when Traversals are badly set up but the roles are inhabited by people with sophisticated traversing capability, they will try and make it work through sheer force of will and extraordinary effort to compensate for the fragmentation in the Traversal. This is one reason why good people burn out or leave organizations – another hidden cost.

Traversals are the next level of complexity and so getting at the hidden cost is more difficult. It is simply unrealistic and idealistic to expect to have all Traversals working perfectly all the time. However, it is vital to spot the ones that are having the biggest impact on productivity, profitability and performance.

Below we share some case studies that illustrate how Traversals can go awry and create hidden costs.

Case study 1: Customers fall between two teams

Context

To action a discretionary refund, a retailer directed a customer to contact their VAT Refunds team via an instruction at the top of their order confirmation.

Scenario

The VAT Refunds team received the refund request from the customer and sent it on to the Customer Services team to action. After a while, the customer received an email from the Customer Services team telling them they had contacted the wrong department and directing them to contact the VAT Refunds team instead. So the customer was back at the start of the process. This went on for over a year. Every time the customer followed the instructions on the order confirmation to process the refund, they would get an email back telling them to contact the Customer Services team. This would go back and forth like a game of ping pong until the customer called the helpline to resolve the issue.

How the issue with the Traversal showed up

A suboptimal Traversal activity and process are both evident. Both teams have accountability to perform a Traversal activity (customer refunds) as part of the customer journey. The two teams may have slightly different accountabilities – one processing general customer refunds and the other VAT refunds. The activity of processing a discretionary refund, whilst part of the customer journey process, was in a gap. Both teams believed the other to be responsible.

The Traversal activity and process were not clearly defined in the Roles of either team. This was further compounded by a rigid silo as over the course of 12 months many individuals from both teams were unable or unwilling to take the insight provided by the customer and resolve the issue to prevent future occurrences.

From a Behaviours perspective, it's clear neither team had the customer experience in mind as they only followed their part of the process. The rigid silo between the two teams prevented cooperation to resolve the situation.

Customer refunds are a core part of any business and key to a positive customer experience. The hidden cost is significant – not only in multiple instances of rework when many roles touch a simple process but also in reputation and lost revenue as customers choose to save themselves the hassle and go elsewhere.

We can probably all identify with similar experiences and at first glance they may appear trivial. However, issues like these will only continue and the impact will increase exponentially unless they are fixed. More problematically perhaps, in this example, there is an unhelpful dynamic in the organization where there appears to be no broader viewpoint and sense of urgency to solve a fairly simple issue impacting the customer. The lack of interdependence and cooperation to fix the issue will simply perpetuate.

Case Study 2: Fortress business partnering

Context

An organization introduced a matrix structure to drive consistent standards, share expertise across the divisions and prevent cost escalation by sharing specialized roles located in central teams. This was a principle in the Enterprise Organization Blueprint and business partnering was defined as a Traversal activity located in certain roles.

Scenario

Each division had an HR Director (HRD) whose role included business partnering to join up across the matrix. The roles dual reported to the Divisional President and the Chief People Officer. The requirement for the HRD to have a foot in both camps and align both agendas was clear, documented and unambiguous. HRDs were expected to adhere to common standards and access and share expertise from specialist teams. However, one of the divisions behaved as if they were an independent business and acted as though the other areas of the business were below par or got in the way of their progress and performance.

How the issue with the Traversal showed up

Over time the HRD of this division started to share less, cancelled alignment calls, independently performed specialized work, deviated from company processes and even recruited additional specialist roles to supplement the divisional team. The chat became about 'fortresses' and 'going rogue'. All of which introduced hidden cost, for example, duplication, additional headcount and process workarounds.

Despite the fact the business partnering role was an agreed Traversal activity, the HRD was pulled in opposite directions because of the way the division operated as a rigid silo. It's more than likely that the HRD unconsciously skewed the role towards the division in order to survive. Taken individually the Behaviours that showed up weren't significant. However, when noticed and added together, they undermined the principle of the matrix organization.

Case Study 3: Silo working

Context

An organization had a compliance team that worked with nearly every area of the business to ensure it operated within legal and ethical boundaries. For example, they were accountable for embedding operational controls and acting as a sounding board for interpreting new regulations.

Scenario

The compliance lead operated a deeply siloed team with eight layers from the top to the bottom of the team. The team was strongly controlled and decision-making centred at the top.

How the issue with the Traversal showed up

Straightforward, but operationally vital tasks, like applying for approval for regulated roles, were incredibly difficult and slow to progress. Even though there was a defined process in place, multiple interactions were required to get these activities moving and decisions had to go up the hierarchy. Other functions had to have project teams in place to track progress as numerous people from different teams got involved to try and resolve issues and accelerate progress. Work and energy centred around influencing the compliance lead and the chat was often about strategies to make headway. It felt like a game of 'cat and mouse' and degenerated into a game of blame.

This case study illustrates what happens when a Traversal activity, owned by a Traversal area and delivered through a Traversal process, doesn't operate optimally due to a rigid silo. The silo resulted from the 'tone from the top' that pulled the focus of the compliance team to be internal and up, rather than looking out and working across organization boundaries to coordinate an operationally vital process. The excessive control over decision-making made the process cumbersome and drew in too many people as they tried to break through the silo to get information and sway the leader to make a decision.

Summary

Traversals in all their guises are essential, as they foster cross-boundary working in organizations. Effective Traversals are both the Constructs that enable work to be done smoothly across the organization and the cooperative Behaviours required for Interdependence. When looking at OE it's useful to prioritize the Traversals that matter strategically, so they can be optimized.

Sub-optimal Traversals appear when people identify too strongly with a boundary in the system – whether it is an activity, area or process – and naturally occurring silos become rigid. There will always be situations where people don't cross boundaries, and this will show up in Behaviours. If the silos harden, we need to decide how significant the hidden costs are to determine what action should be taken.

We can take a lesson from the octopus. Octopuses have prehensile arms, they can move independently to explore, mate, hunt and crawl in any direction. The arms are also linked to its central brain, so the octopus can make these independent arms work together, for example to swim. It's this trick shot that Traversals aim to do in an organization context – enable independence and interdependence to join up activity across boundaries.

Chapter 7
Fault Lines

In geology, fault lines occur as the Earth's crust moves due to tectonic stress. If tension builds up along a fault and then is suddenly released, the result is an earthquake. As we know this causes significant displacement across large volumes of rock and creates a physical separation that has a significant impact on the geology of the area. This metaphor perfectly illustrates the depth and consequence, in terms of cost and stress for people in the system, if divisive organization Fault Line issues are left unattended.

What is a Fault Line?

Organizations are organized in some way by principles and boundaries which are sometimes unspoken and sometimes defined. The critical principles and boundaries, around which everything else needs to be organized, sit in an Enterprise Operating Charter. These principles and boundaries need to be aligned to the Vision & Strategy of the organization. Once they are aligned leaders need to hold to the principles and boundaries at an enterprise level, to ensure the system is resilient and holds steady under pressure. When decisions are made or avoided, or strategies evolve such that these principles and boundaries become misaligned, they devolve into Fault Lines. This is why Fault Lines impact the whole system, including how Roles and Traversals function effectively. They result from misalignment at the enterprise level, specifically in the Enterprise Operating Charter (EOC) or the Enterprise Organization Blueprint (EOrB) levels of the OE Spine. It's these particular boundaries and principles we are most interested in here.

To explore this further, let's use our marine analogy. Silfra, in Iceland, is the only place in the world where you can dive or snorkel directly in a crack between two tectonic plates. From land the Silfra fissure looks like a small channel of water. The fissure only becomes visible after you have donned your drysuit and very slowly immersed yourself in the arctic water. In an organization context, a planned, slow and deliberate exploration of the OE issue will help leaders to understand what is going on. When people snorkel over Silfra, they report getting vertigo, the dizzying sensation that they are moving when they are not – feeling like they are falling over a cliff or being unable to move. In an organization a Fault Line creates confusion and slows delivery. The Silfra fissure goes deep. As you swim and float on the surface it is hard to see the bottom or the overall shape of it. In an organization a Fault Line can also be difficult to see. We know it's there, but it's hard to get a sense of the shape. Consequently, we often apply superficial solutions to Fault Line issues, such as assuming a talented individual can fix a Fault Line alone. Silfra was formed by the divergent tectonic drift of the Eurasian and North American plates and they continue to drift about 2cm farther apart every year, building up tension which is relieved through periodic major earthquakes. Geological Fault Lines are created from the tension and worsen as friction builds. When there is a Fault Line in an organization it will have the same effect.

Silfra looks beautiful. At some point in recent or ancient history, boundaries and principles will have been deliberately designed into the organization. At the time they will have looked reasonable and may well have been the best course of action. They could perhaps even have been 'beautiful'. However, if an enterprise evolves in response to its environment, but fails to regularly re-align the organization to changes over time, the impact into the system can become significant. The organization system then has to weather the Fault Lines that develop. Fault Lines will exist as a result of commercial decisions, mergers and acquisitions, old ways of working versus new ways of working, the introduction of new technology, different frames of reference between leaders and more often than not, when decisions have been avoided or haven't been aligned down the system.

The key point is that as organizations evolve, they are likely to develop Fault Lines due to the failure or lag in aligning the rest of the system to changes, especially those at enterprise level. When newer organization Constructs are designed on a Fault Line, they are inevitably unstable and have movement underneath. What we may notice is friction or tension between people inhabiting Roles, but if the Roles sit on a Fault Line what is actually going on is organizational 'tectonic plates' moving against each other. Left unchecked, they will eventually rupture. Everyone knows when a Fault Line exists – we can feel it. Confusion caused by Fault Lines can show up in any role and will cause issues with the organization model, structure, roles, processes, information flow and decision making. All of this costs the company on the bottom line through lost productivity, retention of key staff, lower discretionary effort and friction between people leading to an uncomfortable working environment.

Common examples of Fault Lines

- When businesses grow big enough to need economies of scale and consistent policies and processes, or grow so big that they introduce global approaches, they create new boundaries that can become Fault Lines.
  Example: Global category or shared services functions that set new boundaries and principles around where work gets done. These changes can become Fault Lines if the Enterprise Organization Blueprint fails to align the accountabilities, connectivity and decision rights across the organization.
- When specific strategic choices cause Fault Lines because the Charter or Blueprint are out of kilter for a period of time.

Example: Mergers and acquisitions prior to full integration, internal startups like incubators, strategic transformations or the creation of new business units or new functions.

- When strategy changes and an original source of advantage is no longer applicable.
  Example: A strategic partnership or outsourcing arrangement that the organization is contractually committed to, but which no longer aligns to the new strategic direction.

- When organizations use the concept of internal profit and loss centres or internal recharging in order to create a commercial focus and see how much the product or output actually costs to produce. This approach has its merits but it also creates boundaries that can become Fault Lines.
  Example: Internal units measured on the health of their P&L do not focus on required activity unless they can charge the cost to another internal P&L centre.

- Organizing parts of a business around people and favourite 'Crewmates' can create Fault Lines.
  Example: When roles are not designed around the work but created as a result of a personal relationship. This can create a Fault Line because the individual may not have the capabilities required to further the strategy or has power by association to act independently outside the Enterprise Organization Blueprint boundaries or principles.

So, you may be thinking, if it's so common and arguably unavoidable, why do we care about Fault Lines? It's just life and reality. It will always be the case, as the external or internal context evolves, that boundaries change, principles are altered, leaders move and so on. To some extent it is, but there are also very real reasons why Fault Lines are best managed. Using our marine metaphor, if we don't handle the Fault Line it is like an octopus clouding the water with ink. The ink is an irritant; it has a bad taste and a bad smell. In an organization Fault Lines create confusion, a lack of traction, repetition of work and swirling – all of which adds cost and angst into the system. Leaders will, to some extent, be distanced from the very real friction that is created as the Fault Lines move. Ultimately, Fault Lines may lead to impossible jobs that people can't fathom, or Constructs designed to manage the confusion that have the effect of slowing down pace. An octopus will die if exposed to its own ink for a long period of time and an organization is no different – talent leaves, there will be a negative impact on the P&L and there may be reputational damage.

When there is a Fault Line the organization and its people have to cope with the impact of the misalignment. They create Constructs, like meetings, excessive governance or additional teams that generate Behaviours that are trying to mitigate the impact of the Fault Line but in reality add significant hidden costs. Inevitably this situation will have a disproportionate impact on productivity, profitability and performance as people are using energy, time and focus to hold the organization in place across a Fault Line. This creates massive friction which often shows up as blame, silos, internal focus, over-control or a diversion into simplistic solutions. People are being distracted.

Why do Fault Lines exist in organizations?

We've said this book is about money and fish. Fault Lines are a great example of where we don't pay enough attention to the money wrapped up in the fish. As leaders, our focus is necessarily on financial and commercial matters and we tend to pay less attention to addressing the Fault Lines in our organization. Earlier chapters introduced some of the reasons for this in terms of the limitations of our frames of reference, a tendency to avoid examining the system and our instinct to protect the status quo. We've always found diagnosing the existence of Fault Lines is a 'go slow, to go fast' moment as they are extraordinarily challenging. We explore this in some depth in the case studies below.

There are no absolutes in OE, but generally Fault Lines will have their origins in the top half of the OE Spine at the Enterprise Operating Charter (EOC) and Enterprise Organization Blueprint (EOrB) level. This is because they are the pivot point in our OE Spine, where the concepts of the Vision & Strategy start to meet real life. More often than not we find Fault Lines show up at the EOrB level. The EOrB translates the conceptual Vision & Strategy and high level EOC principles and boundaries into the reality of an integrated configuration of how all the work required to deliver the strategy is organized. It is the bridge between concept and reality. It is the high-level design that draws out how the work of the whole organization fits together. If you were going to build a boat or a submarine, you would demand a detailed blueprint, with clear specifications for every part, to ensure it worked as a whole and the outcome was seaworthy and fit for its intended purpose.

This notion of concept and reality is an interesting one and could go some way to understanding why Fault Lines show up and why they are not dealt with. Concepts like Vision & Strategy live in the realm of ideas – by their nature they are intangible, flexible and incomplete. Reality, in an organizational context, demands specificity, if it is to align to the boundaries and principles defined by the Charter. Reality in this sense, is also where a conceptual idea can be judged to have succeeded or failed.

Although we may not like to admit it, in this context, we generally prefer the safety of possibility over the vulnerability of reality. It might be worth thinking about this idea because most of us would say we are all about reality – being concrete and pragmatic. But there is an Ink Cloud that is obscuring what's going on.

Possibility often feels safer because it allows us to remain in our comfort zone, sidestep change and avoid being pinned down to the commitment required to align to the principles and boundaries within the Charter and the Blueprints. By keeping our options open, we can resist transparency and shield ourselves from genuine challenge. We can be seen to be delivering even though we may be working from personal agendas or perpetuating the status quo. In this way, possibility becomes a protective cloak, enabling pseudo-alignment that looks like agreement but lacks real substance. Pragmatism, too, can slip into a shallow mode that can lead to simplistic fixes rather than engaging in the deeper, more demanding thinking that true progress requires.

Reality, on the other hand, is vulnerable because it must be clear, unambiguous and transparent – open for all to see, rigorously thought through and aligned with the enterprise's boundaries and principles so that action becomes unambiguous. It demands commitment, forces choices between competing options and requires the rejection or loss of alternatives. Yet when we fail to anchor concrete action within those boundaries and principles, we risk creating Fault Lines that undermine alignment and expose the organization to fracture.

There are also other broader challenges because translating ideas into reality requires imagination, planning and practical steps – often not the skill set of a single person. We often underestimate the mental energy or levels of collaboration required to move from 'what if' to 'how to'. Fault Lines are particularly problematic in this zone as: what is required to translate ideas into reality is overlooked; complexity catches us off guard; or we reach for simplistic solutions sending us down the wrong path.

Fault Lines tend to exist in areas of the organization that are messy, ambiguous or scary. We often avoid them as they can be too tricky to fathom or approach. For example, some Fault Lines favour particular senior leaders and as a result they are unwilling to acknowledge or address them. Sometimes, simply the perception that influential people are wedded to their perspective makes it hard to examine Fault Lines and leaves an unhelpful status quo in place. This can happen even though everyone knows a Fault Line exists. In each case, the status quo masks a Fault Line, which, like tectonic plates, continue to rub against each other. Eventually they will rupture. In the meantime they will certainly be costing the organization money.

In the case studies below we illustrate some common Fault Lines. There is no doubt Fault Lines generate cost in the system. By their nature they are intensely complex, embedded and require resources and effort to examine, address and implement any changes. It's very difficult and time consuming to try and fully quantify the costs of a Fault Line. This is because you would need to work out the cost of it remaining, the cost of removing it and the cost of the unknown impact of it staying in place (or not). It's a core dilemma for every CEO. However, given the significant impact of Fault Lines on an organization, and despite all the obstacles that will inevitably get in the way, the true nature of Fault Lines needs to be thoroughly explored and understood so you can make more informed choices about whether the effort is worth the prize.

Understanding Fault Lines

We've mentioned above a few of the clues to identifying Fault Lines, like areas of the business that are overtly messy, ambiguous or scary or camouflage Behaviours that could be holding the status quo in place. Like Silfra, what you first see doesn't reveal whether a Fault Line exists or – if it does – what shape it is. This complexity means that you need to pause, stand back and use the OE Spine in the Model to see if it's a Fault Line that is creating or building tension. We will demonstrate this approach in our case studies.

The OE Spine depicts how the organization system aligns. It will help us to locate the organization Fault Lines. When we are looking for Fault Lines we are assuming that there is a Vision & Strategy and that it is fit for purpose. If they are not in place or not fit for purpose, then you need to start here before you attempt to locate Fault Lines. Our focus here is on the Charter and Enterprise Blueprint alignment to the Vision & Strategy.

Below are some case studies to bring this alive. As a reminder, the case studies are a fusion from many different organizations to ensure anonymity. When looking for the origin of a Fault Line the approach is the same. A Fault Line always starts with a Construct so we start by looking at the base of the OE Spine – with insights on Roles. From there we go up the OE Spine as far as the Unit Organization Blueprint – if the issue is still evident we need to go to the top of the OE Spine and work down from the Vision & Strategy to trace what's causing the Fault Line.

Case study 1: Insights

Scenario

An organization introduced a Vision & Strategy to sell customized products and services. One year into this new strategic direction, the marketing function was under increasing pressure to create the products and services that would generate breakthrough growth. The Chief Information Technology Officer (CIO) had been in office for over 12 years and enjoyed significant power and influence. We would call him an 'Anchor Weight'.

How the issue showed up

There was significant friction between the marketing and IT functions. There were similar roles in the structures of both functions. The people inhabiting those roles were at loggerheads with each other. There also appeared to be a personality clash between the marketing leader, who blamed IT for poor quality data and the IT leader who blamed Marketing for demanding excessive data in unrealistic timeframes.

Understanding the Fault Line

Using the OE Spine we can track up the bottom half and then down from the top half to see where the Fault Line originates.

Role level – We know the issue was showing up in both IT and marketing data roles and appeared to be the people inhabiting roles who didn't get along. However, the messiness across both functions and the presence of camouflage Behaviours, 'Eddies' and 'Ink Clouds' in particular, indicate a potential Fault Line.

Unit Organization Design level – The IT Data Shared Services team produced monthly customer sales and other customer data reports. Marketing had a team focused on receiving all the data available on customers, competitors and market trends and turning them into actionable strategies to guide product development. So the Unit Organization Designs looked like they were organized to deliver their respective buckets of work.

Unit Organization Blueprint level – Continuing to track up the OE Spine, both the IT and marketing functions had defined a detailed view of the buckets of work required to deliver their functional data accountabilities.

So far, both functions had what you would expect to see. However, the ongoing friction leads us to think there is a Fault Line further up the OE Spine.

We now go to the top of the OE Spine and work down.

Vision & Strategy level – The Vision & Strategy exists and is fit for purpose and the customization strategy is clear.

Before going any further we need to understand how we might pinpoint the Fault Line. We know the issue is showing up in data roles and teams. We also know that a customization strategy requires a particular approach to data as it depends on variation rather than aggregation. To generate insights there needs to be the ability to blend customer-centric, behavioural and operational data alongside other insights to develop products and services. It would be helpful to hold this in mind as we continue through the case study.

Enterprise Operating Charter (EOC) level – The business model was agreed five years ago and included a principle that clustered all things data together as part of its focus on achieving economies of scale. It predated the customization Vision & Strategy and was an established Construct. Over time, through implicit agreement, the IT function became the custodian of data, either because of its close link to the technology infrastructure or as an extension of its established responsibilities for data security, compliance, and risk governance.

Enterprise Organization Blueprint (EOrB) level – Five years ago shared services were set up to realize the EOC principle of economies of scale. These shared service teams were set up as a single unit to serve multiple teams across the business.

The IT function provided data to all parts of the organization from the Data Shared Services team. This meant that they standardized processes and executed routine transactional tasks (e.g. the monthly data reports).

This is the point *where the concept* of data production *meets the reality* of doing the actual work and we start to be curious. Would a shared service doing a repeatable standardized activity be focused on delivering a customization strategy? What is the nature of the friction between IT and Marketing?

When reviewed further it was evident that the IT shared services were continuing to operate in line with the original clustering principle and the shared services blueprint design. This meant they largely provided the same customer data reports they always had rather than adapting to the newer customization strategy. If they'd adapted we would expect to see them provide raw data in the format required for the Marketing Insight team or an enhanced shared service offer that produced the blended insights required to enable a marketing team to turn it into customized products and services.

In this case study, the OE Spine has fractured at the Enterprise Blueprint (EOrB) level because a newer organization Construct (customization strategy) has been introduced over the top of existing Constructs (the Charter principles of data clustering and shared services). *These are the organization 'tectonic plates' that are causing the rupture*. The IT function may be experienced as being awkward but in reality there are opposing organization 'tectonic plates' that are simultaneously holding them in place and requiring them to change. The leaders definitely had options on how to handle this. Nevertheless, the experience of the people in both teams was of friction and confusion.

What might have been holding the Fault Line in place

The complexity of this situation could have been exacerbated by the presence of many other Constructs, Behaviours and Interplays holding this Fault Line in place. For example:

- There may have been a lack of understanding about the implications of a customization strategy from the perspective of all disciplines, for example, in terms of budget and investment.
- The IT function may not have been allocated additional budget to support changes in resources or to develop customization capabilities.
- The IT function may have been grappling with legacy technology that wasn't fit for purpose.
- It's possible that the CIO and his leadership team were still being rewarded for standardized and cost-effective delivery.

- Given the CIO's time in post it may have been hard for anyone to probe or examine the issue or change structures, roles and capabilities, with such a powerful leader holding the status quo in place.
- Because of the level of frustration within and between the two functions, silos will have developed with unhelpful frames of reference on both sides that prevented cooperation.

The need to handle data in a different way to deliver the new customization strategy had fractured at the Enterprise Blueprint level because no-one had paid attention to the implicit agreements or the need to actively adapt the clustering and economies of scale principles at the Enterprise Charter level. There was a need to really think through and make sense of what was required to translate a concept into reality, into roles that could do optimal work. The Charter and the Enterprise Blueprint had been overlooked.

The hidden costs in this case study are significant. They include the lost opportunity to drive the strategy and generate new sources of revenue, the resource, effort and time spent trying to get the data into a format that was useful, the duplication of activity or shadow Roles, the time spent in meetings discussing what was going wrong and the 'Eddies' and blame resulting from the silos.

Case Study 2: Decision rights

Scenario

A global organization implemented a new strategy to drive upper quartile performance. This strategy required improvement in both revenue growth and margin. The strategy defined four product categories and heralded the implementation of a new 'globally directed, regionally managed' organization.

How the issue showed up

Friction showed up at different times and at various levels, between the global category team, the regions and the local markets. Initially, it was in isolated teams, with predictable tension around brand decisions – for example, product discontinuation and brand positioning. During the course of the annual planning process the friction increased as both the global category and the regional teams presented conflicting brand plans. Versions of the same conversation were replayed at every meeting.

Some people were at loggerheads with each other, whereas others were not. It didn't seem to follow a pattern but it was clear that the matrix dual reporting of the category leads wasn't fostering collaboration across the organization. There was 'water cooler' chat from the regions that the category model was not workable in this type of organization. There were also data driven attempts to discredit category strategies, for example, by showing how a particular approach to brand packaging couldn't work in a particular market. There was also 'water cooler' chat from the global category team that the regions were 'dinosaurs', refusing to collaborate or cooperate and again data driven attempts to discredit them.

Over time the friction was so strong you could almost feel it, and it was showing up at every level including C-suite.

Understanding the Fault Line

Again, using the OE Spine we can track up from the bottom half and then down from the top half to see where the Fault Line originates.

Role level – Similar to the Insights case study the issue was showing up at the base of the OE Spine and appeared to be the people inhabiting Roles, at different levels in the organization who didn't get along. However, the presence of ambiguity on decisions like brand plans, as well as camouflage Behaviours, like 'Eddies' and 'Ink Clouds', indicated a potential Fault Line.

Unit Organization Design level – Each category lead had a team responsible for strategy, innovation, insights and brand management.

Unit Organization Blueprint level – The global category team was organized into the four product categories. The category leads were senior functional Roles and dual reported in the matrix to the Global Category President and one of the regional Presidents. This approach was introduced to encourage collaboration and connection across the business.

So far so good. However, the ongoing friction leads us to think there is a Fault Line further up the OE Spine. We now go to the top of the OE Spine and work down.

Vision & Strategy level – The communication and messaging around the 'globally directed, regionally led' Vision & Strategy was clear. It outlined the potential impact on both the Constructs and Behaviours and was specific about the need to achieve a stronger brand identity, category leadership, stronger functions and economies of scale from product rationalization and shared assets.

Before going any further we need to understand how we might pinpoint the Fault Line. In this case study, the reality required to enable the Vision & Strategy is that the global functions needed to be able to set the parameters for the rest of the organization. From a category point of view examples might be the innovation pipeline itself, global brand characteristics, market share targets, price positioning, gross margin or product rationalization.

Hold that in the back of your mind as we work down the OE Spine.

Enterprise Operating Charter (EOC) level – The Strategy to drive both growth and margin improvement required a significant change in all parts of the Enterprise Operating Charter. The Charter articulated the Constructs and Behaviours that would enable the organization to be 'globally directed, regionally managed', for example, outlining activities like manufacturing that would be centralized to a single global function to drive economies of scale.

Enterprise Organization Blueprint (EOrB) level – As a result of the change in strategy, a new global category team with decision rights to drive global category strategy and innovation and to act as custodians of the global brands in four category areas was created. Prior to this change each Region had been accountable for defining their own product strategies, innovation plans and changing brand elements, even on global brands, to suit local needs. To instill and reinforce the new collaborative Behaviours that were needed, the organization formalized a matrix organization with all senior functional Roles dual reporting with a *solid line to the function Executive and dotted line to the Region President*. So, for senior functional Roles the primary decision-maker was clearly with the function Executive.

> However, there was an *anomaly* with the global category team. The decision to shift the power from the regional Presidents to the Global Category President was highly sensitive. So, to try and manage the change and 'soften the blow' the category leads were allocated *dual solid* reporting lines. They each reported to the Global Category President and one of the regional Presidents. *The reporting lines were of equal weight*. The rationale used was to create a sense of everyone being 'in it together' and accountable, and to provide reassurance to the Region Presidents that they still had influence.

This is the point *where a concept meets reality*. Given all the friction we need to start to be curious. Is the nature of the friction related to the global teams setting parameters for the rest of the organization? Is it a result of the reporting anomaly in the EOrB? Does this dual solid reporting line fail to reinforce the required shift?

When reviewed, the Fault Line shows up at the Enterprise Blueprint level around the choice to have dual solid reporting lines for the global category team. It was not clear at the C-Suite who the primary decision maker was between the regional Presidents and the Global Category President, even though the accountabilities had ostensibly moved to the global category team. The global category team dual reporting lines had been designed to avoid dealing with the sensitive shift at C-Suite level.

In this case study, the tensions around power flowed down the organization and created impossible jobs, not only in centralized global category teams, but also in Manufacturing, regional teams and the local markets.

What might have been holding the Fault Line in place?

The complexity of this situation was exacerbated by the fear of disruption to revenue and margin that might have occurred by following through too quickly on the shift in decision making power that the strategy required. Other factors holding it in place were:

- The Construct around category decision-making was unclear as decision-making was not owned in one place.
- Unlike other centralized functions the global category team could not set the parameters and clarify the Behaviours expected of each part of the business in a global approach.
- Legacy Behaviours were able to continue as the regions still had considerable influence (via the dual solid reporting line) on aspects like innovation, product rationalization, manufacturing and other key areas.

- It is also likely that relationships were being protected.

The hidden costs in this case study are again significant. They include the delay in implementing interventions to drive improvement in both revenue growth and margin, the continuation of old ways of working driving decisions that had to be unpicked and of course the friction between senior people that became widespread across multiple geographies and functions and permeated relationships. This lack of pace, productivity and agility perpetuated. As the issue became more divisive, leaders avoided making structural or people decisions which further compounded the issue.

Summary

Just like Silfra, Fault Lines can look 'beautiful' on the surface. However, below the waterline, Fault Lines are 'stuffed to the gunwales' with every hidden cost, as we've previously outlined. Fault Lines need to be spotted, examined and consciously handled.

By first, identifying that a Fault Line exists, then understanding its true nature, including what might be holding it in place, we can take a deliberate approach that avoids unintended consequences and costs. There are instances when choosing to create a Fault Line or hold one in place for a time is necessary. A good example of this would be mergers and acquisition or internal restructuring. However, for every day that a Fault Line is in place, the organization is at risk of the tectonic plates rupturing. While they exist, Fault Lines create internal friction, distractions and perpetuate hidden costs that hit the bottom line.

Chapter 8
Currents

From culture to Currents

Before we get to Currents, we need to talk about culture. It's widely accepted that organization culture has a significant impact on the long-term economic performance of a business. For example, culture can enable a rapid, coordinated response to fight a competitor or help to realize major change. Culture is never static and it has powerful consequences that can even determine the success or failure of a business.

As we are focused on diagnosing the issues that are getting in the way of OE, culture will inevitably be part of the equation. However, here's the rub – the *word* 'culture' holds within it the highly complex, multi-facetted and difficult to define *nature* of culture. The way we tend to think about culture can get in the way of us clearly examining our organization systems. There are three aspects we'd like to highlight:

- **Definition of 'culture'** – If you look up a definition of 'culture', it encompasses a whole host of elements including: beliefs, assumptions, values, norms, symbols, language, traditions, rituals, actions, interactions and more. It's held in place by norms and social reinforcement, including fear of penalties or exclusion. It's tied to identity, institutional structures, fear of uncertainty, inter-generational transmission and so on. It's extraordinarily complex and multi-dimensional.

- **The word 'culture'** – We use the word 'culture' to mean all sorts of things: ways of working, value statements, informal rules or even as a judgement on unacceptable Behaviours – 'It's a culture issue'. The word 'culture' is often used as shorthand for everything that's going on that can't be explained or is too difficult to be examined. 'Culture' can become an 'Ink Cloud' in the system to avoid addressing tricky issues. It can also be over-simplified and boiled down to single ideas like teamwork or empowerment without really understanding the meaning or dynamics that lie beneath. Sometimes it's even used to indicate compliance with corporate governance requirements.

- **Culture as a catch-all** – 'Culture' is sometimes used as a catch-all to avoid facing reality – 'It's the culture that's getting in our way'. Similar to Fault Lines, culture exists in that problematic zone between concept and reality. As a result we may overlook the myriad Constructs, Behaviours and Interplays which are influencing the culture.

Over the years, a single word has been used with many different meanings, to encompass many different issues and this has clouded the reality of this massively complex phenomenon.

The complexity of culture is the reason it's so difficult to change. We'll all have experienced different culture change initiatives over the course of our careers. Here are some examples, using our definition of OE, to illustrate different approaches to culture change with varying degrees of success.

- An organization defined its values and Behaviours in line with its Vision & Strategy. They then had a big launch with pop-up spaces, banners, giveaways and merchandise. This was reinforced by posters in all the meeting rooms and kitchens and with screensavers (Constructs). They expected colleagues to behave differently but the status quo culture continued.
- An organization with a matrix structure implemented business partner Roles (Constructs) to enable its stated core value of collaboration (Behaviours). They also invested in developing capabilities and encouraged cooperation and cross-boundary working (Behaviours). Simultaneously, the CEO had implicit agreements with certain business units to be autonomous (Constructs and Behaviours). Two different Interplays clashed and created a sense of dissonance in the culture.

It is important to articulate and encourage the kind of Behaviours needed in an organization and we'd expect to see standards that set expectations as part of the Enterprise

Operating Charter in our OE Spine. Yet it's not enough to simply define Behaviours. Behaviours are only part of what's really going on. The Behaviours needed to fulfill the Vision & Strategy will only show up if they are shaped and reinforced through every Construct in the system. The Constructs and Behaviours create the Interplays which generate the culture. There will always be too many Interplays to be able to see each one or to pinpoint all the causal linkages between specific Constructs and Behaviours. However, to illustrate the dynamic clearly, we've isolated one example in a simplified way.

- A multi-national company implemented a reward system to drive enterprise performance and foster collaboration across business units by encouraging specific leadership Behaviours. The reward system continued to be heavily focused towards the delivery of business outcomes, but leaders' Behaviours were also evaluated using specific Constructs, the outcome of which materially impacted their discretionary pay – if leaders didn't meet the required behavioural standards, no matter their business performance, their bonus would be zero (Constructs). Over a couple of years this impacted leaders' Behaviours, for example leaders made decisions or took actions for the enterprise that were not necessarily purely in their own interests. Over time, this Interplay contributed to a collaborative culture and had a positive impact on business performance.

In every system, the culture can get in the way of spotting and addressing OE issues. Instead of trying to 'boil the ocean', the 3D-OE Diagnostic Framework™ takes you on a step-by-step journey to illuminate the aspects of your culture that are impacting your OE. At each stage the approach supports you to see the various Constructs and Behaviours and helps you to keep in mind that there are Interplays going on that are holding the issues in place. Throughout the Process, the accumulated patterns of all the Interplays begin to show up as repeated themes. If the culture is the whole ocean, what we are focused on are the Currents – the accumulated patterns within the culture that are really getting in the way of OE. This is what makes our approach different. It enables you to cut through the complexity to understand the Currents that are getting in the way of the OE issues you are examining. This offers you a direct and effective way to unlock meaningful improvements in productivity, profitability and performance in your business.

What are Currents?

Ocean currents are ongoing, directed movements of seawater. They are held in place by a combination of forces – wind, temperature, salinity, gravity and tides. They move water horizontally and vertically across vast distances. Currents in organizations are similar. They are ongoing and pervasive patterns within a system that are generated and then held in place by the 'accumulated forces' from the Interplays between Constructs and Behaviours. They are unique to a particular system.

There are several different classifications of ocean current including surface, deep, upwelling, downwelling and tidal, that are primarily created and influenced by different forces and move seawater in different directions. In organizations, Currents influence the habits or patterns of working in all directions across the system, for example, where information has to flow up to the top of the hierarchy for a decision to be made.

Ocean currents are also vital to regulate global climate, transport, heat and move nutrients and gases throughout the ocean. They aid navigation and the speed of shipping around the world. In organizations, Currents are equally important to enable the smooth flow of work, facilitate productivity and speed and can regulate the organization's capacity to function optimally and grow. However, some Currents develop that hinder the flow of work and slow things down or propel an organization in an unforeseen direction, both of which create hidden cost or impede performance.

Understanding Currents

The idea of 'accumulated forces' that flow from the Interplays between Constructs and Behaviours goes some way to explain the strength of the system. They are the paradigms we talked about in Chapter 1 that influence how we feel, think and behave in our organization. This is why in our Diagnostic Model we depict Currents as dynamic arrows flowing around everything in the Model – influenced by and influencing the OE Spine.

We will always be facing a myriad of Constructs, Behaviours and Interplays that are holding the status quo in place. Recognizing the strength of the system in terms of these combined forces, should give us pause, at least for a moment, before trying to change things. If we can hold the idea that we are, in essence, taking on the system when we attempt to do this, then it becomes clear that the choices we make to influence organizational effectiveness need to be grounded in deep insight, thoughtfully designed and enacted through reinforcing interventions. What we choose to do needs to address all three active elements – Constructs, Behaviours and the Interplay between them – to have any chance of influencing or re-directing the 'accumulated forces'. For example, we have seen organizations deploy interventions that successfully re-directed the energy being spent on blaming others across silo boundaries, into cooperation and collaboration.

Like the sea, organization Currents move energy around the system. They are not always predictable; they may take you somewhere fast or prevent you getting there. It's generally easier to go with organization Currents than fight against them. We all get caught up in Currents because we are part of the system. Sometimes, it's like getting caught in a rip current which you can't always spot and will take you miles out to sea. The coastguard's advice would always be not to fight it, float and breathe to get your bearings, then to move sideways out of the rip. So, for us to be able to examine Currents we need to pause, get our bearings and move out of the flow. This is what the Framework helps us to do by stepping through the layers of complexity so we can start to see the Currents that are impacting the OE issues we are examining.

The Currents that are generated in any organization will be unique and the nuances of how they show up will vary. Below we explore three common organization Currents – Rush Current, Control Current and Blame Current.

Rush Current

The Rush Current is dominant in most organizations and can be linked to the 'Goals at all cost' frames of reference we covered in Chapter 1. It is a pervasive pattern of rushing to action that prevents leaders being '*willing and able*' to get under the surface of the OE issues. This Current is like the North Atlantic Gulf Stream – it's powerful and fast and has wide-spread influence on weather patterns, climate, eco-systems and shipping routes on both sides of the Atlantic. We've used this example to show how a Current can create headwinds for addressing OE issues and accessing hidden costs.

What is observed

There is a strong emphasis on action as people jump quickly into doing. Activity, output and task completion are rewarded. Thinking, reflection, concept development and time spent working things out are discounted and seen to be 'wasting time'. Decisiveness is valued more than the quality of decision-making. There is a strong focus on deadlines. Communication tends to follow the quickest route, such as messaging platforms or email, with little or no time spent on sense-making or shared understanding.

Understanding the Current through the 3D-OE Diagnostic Framework™

When an organization rushes past complexity or around difficult organizational effectiveness challenges, the true nature of the OE issues remains unexamined. This Current could impact our willingness to find the time and make the effort to use the Framework at all. The need to pause, reflect and 'go slow, to go fast' will feel counterintuitive – as if we are doing something wrong because what is valued is action and speed. Even if we use the Framework, the Current may still influence us to rush to action without pausing to really apply the insight to develop systemic solutions. When we don't have the time or opportunity to really think through challenges because of time pressures in the system, there is less likelihood that we will expand our frames of reference to become aware of the broader issues that are getting in the way of OE.

What's the impact?

As the OE issues remain largely unexamined, it's likely that both stagnation and expediency will occur and the resulting simplistic solutions will give the illusion of progress. Strategic thinking and aligning to clear organizational priorities can suffer. People may lack understanding or alignment with the Vision & Strategy because they move straight to action. When key elements of the organization's OE Spine are missing or misaligned, Fault Lines may appear, Traversals may become sub-optimal and Roles may be challenging to perform. Organization effectiveness issues will form Eddies and little or no time is spent helping people make sense of challenges in the organization. Outputs are prioritized over outcomes and thinking things through before acting is not valued. As a result, people often become overloaded with full diaries, endless task lists and no time to prioritize – leading to stress and overwhelm. A common example is a large transformation programme that's going off track, yet instead of examining why, it's pushed through endless rounds of re-budgeting.

A Rush Current results in all the costs associated with stagnation and expediency as we've examined in Chapter 2, because OE issues remain largely unresolved.

Control Current

This is when there is a pervasive pattern of control around decision-making, including permission to take action, resulting in low trust.

What is observed

What will generally be observed is that decision-making moves up the hierarchy and even small issues escalate. People don't experience downward delegation of authority and actions are slow to move through the system. What we experience is that people from other areas won't act unless they have been told to do so by their leader. Senior leaders are frequently pulled down into detailed, operational problem-solving. We may hear things like: 'It is what it is'; 'There's no point'; 'It's just how things are'; 'I need to check with…'; 'I can't get anyone to…'.

Understanding the Current through the 3D-OE Diagnostic Framework™

Control Currents are closely connected to sub-optimal Traversals. Traversal activities, areas and processes flow through an organization so if there is low trust, they will slow down decision-making and action. If Traversals are not enabled by cooperative Behaviours that build trust, rigid silos will form. When this happens, to compensate for the lack of trust, we put in place controls to manage outcomes or overreach. This is further exacerbated when the Roles involved are not given proper authority. For example, if a CFO doesn't trust other parts of the business to control spending they may require the procurement function to set a low spend limit in the procurement policy. We've seen this having the effect of forcing functions to seek competitive quotes, even for ongoing outsourcing activity with existing strategic partners.

What's the impact?

When this happens, organizations slow down because everyone looks upward for direction and decisions – they have to handle and live with bureaucracy. Colleagues learn not to take initiative and instead wait to be told what to do. They do not have the permission to address OE issues. Power accumulates at the top, creating a bottleneck where progress depends on senior leaders' availability to make decisions. Leaders may be perceived as micro-managing and decisions often require multiple meetings because nothing can be resolved in the moment. Meetings become overcrowded as a way of compensating for unclear authority. Frustration grows across the organization, communication breaks down across hierarchical layers and structures become top-heavy as the assumption takes hold that only leaders can run the business. The hierarchy often has multiple layers and decisions have to travel through the layers to get to the top. Overall this can fuel an 'us and them' dynamic, disempower people and deprive them of the space and autonomy they need to contribute effectively.

Most of the costs outlined in the Roles and Traversals chapters are likely to be present. For example, highly paid leaders doing lower operational work, duplication, reduced productivity, loss of pace, 'Eddies' and multiple meetings.

Blame Current

This is when there is a pervasive pattern of defensive Behaviours that shows up in multiple places, in all sorts of people.

What is observed?

What will generally be observed is that people often shift responsibility away from themselves and onto others. We may hear comments like: 'It's because X didn't do Y', or 'If only that area had done XYZ properly, we'd be able to...' or 'they didn't respond', or 'if something goes wrong, we always get the blame'. People prefer to point fingers and blame other leaders, teams or functions instead of starting to examine the issue from a neutral perspective. They are often inadvertently identifying issues with Roles and Traversals.

Understanding the Current through the 3D-OE Diagnostic Framework™

Blame Currents stem from Fault Lines. As we've said earlier, Fault Lines will impact Traversals and Roles, preventing them from working optimally and will hold rigid silos in place. Fault Lines are fractures in the alignment of the OE Spine so the tension will always lead to ruptures. As the Constructs and Behaviours develop to hold the organization together over the Fault Line, people sense that things aren't functioning properly, that it's hard to do their jobs and they have a strong conviction that they are not at fault. This is understandable as the source of the issue is the fracture in the OE Spine above them. The psychology behind blame is that we blame others to protect ourselves, to restore a sense of control in an unpredictable situation, to simplify complex issues, to protect our status and as a defence against our fears. When people are not fully aware of the Fault Line or if they are, they are not 'willing and able' to address it, they will learn to blame as part of a survival strategy. Many people are not aware of the Fault Line at all, as their frames of reference are limited by where they are sitting in the organization, but they can feel it. As Fault Lines create ruptures at the Enterprise level the impact is system wide.

What's the impact?

When Fault Lines impact Traversals and Roles, they prevent them from working optimally and can even hold rigid silos in place. In fact, silos may deepen as people find it increasingly difficult to cross boundaries to solve problems together. They retreat into familiar territory and defend their status quo. More energy goes into finding someone else to blame and reinforcing that narrative than into addressing the OE issues. In any system, clear boundaries are necessary, but without cooperation across them, the organization stagnates.

Most of the costs outlined in the Fault Lines chapter will be present. This will include the lost opportunity to capture growth and fully realize the Vision & Strategy of the business.

Summary

We are deliberately choosing to make sense of aspects of the culture through the 3D-OE Diagnostic Framework™. We are channeling our attention and energy onto those Currents that are most likely to make the biggest difference to the OE issues at hand.

Currents will always exist and there will of course be Currents that are positive. Even two of the three Currents described above can be positive in the right circumstances (Rush and Control). These thumb-nail sketches are illustrations of intricate and sophisticated organizational phenomena that can impede OE. In these examples there will be lots of Constructs, Behaviours and Interplays and it's impossible to pinpoint all of them. However, it is possible to make a sensible diagnosis and identify the Currents that are flowing around an OE issue by taking the time to find out what's going on across the organization.

The hidden costs are inevitably an amalgamation of those coming from Roles, Traversals and Fault Lines. We can't emphasize enough the scale of these hidden costs. We all know about compound interest, but here it's the opposite – compound cost. The cumulative effect of repeated costs that build on each other over time.

Part 3
Unlocking performance

Chapter 9
How to use the 3D-OE Diagnostic Process

Throughout the book we have explored the hidden cost of OE issues and their impact on the productivity, profitability and performance of organizations. As we covered in Chapter 4, the 3D-OE Diagnostic Framework™ is composed of a Model and a Process. In this section we share our trade secrets by laying out our Process to use the Model so that you can diagnose your OE issues. Earlier we explored the general tendency in organizations to rush to action. Investing time and energy into the 3D-OE Diagnostic Process is a deliberate '*go slow, to go fast*' choice. Slowing down brings all the associated benefits of widening your frames of reference and ensures your effort cuts through to unlock performance in your organization.

Before we go any further, we thought it would be helpful to describe our frames of reference when we approach an OE issue – it's an important factor in making the application of the Diagnostic successful. We hold in mind and apply anthropological principles. Here are our key ones:

- Take a systemic viewpoint.
- Understand the whole context before reaching conclusions.
- Be curious and avoid assumptions.
- Be comfortable with complexity and ambiguity.
- Listen and pay attention to what's said *and* unsaid.
- Notice patterns that reveal systems of meaning.

Step 1 – Spotting your OE issues

You may already know where your issues are or you may have a sense that your organization isn't quite performing optimally, but like the octopus, the issues are camouflaged and elusive. The first step is to figure out where you start before you deploy the full 3D-OE Diagnostic Framework™. Any diagnostic has implications as it involves resources, time and effort and raises all the messy and uncomfortable challenges associated with examining the status quo. Therefore, it is important to be thoughtful and consider which OE issues you prioritize.

From where you sit in the organization, you will inevitably be seeing things from a particular viewpoint that includes your own frames of reference. You may even be unconsciously holding in place status quo Behaviours. None of us can discern the full materiality of what's going on around us without widening our perspective. It's therefore beneficial, ahead of starting a Diagnostic Process, to brainstorm with your team or even better, a small, diverse group, what you notice in the organization – start to get curious, be aware of what's being said and unsaid. Focusing your conversation around the following two aspects will get you started:

a) Red flag Roles

Role issues are the first red flag as they may be an indicator of more complex OE challenges further up the OE Spine. You are looking for Roles that are regularly discussed, where there is friction between people or where you are observing the camouflage Behaviours that are holding the status quo in place. Here's our approach:

- Brainstorm where 'Eddies' or 'Ink Clouds' appear to be in the system.
- Be open to perceptions of where 'Crewmates' or 'Anchor Weights' may be in play.
- Ensure that people feel they can 'speak truth to power' – this will help you understand how people are making sense of what's going on around them.
- Avoid conflating the Role and the person – issues with Roles could be the Role *or* the person *or* both.

In summary your intention needs to be to explore what's not working and avoid making assumptions. There could very well be capability issues however it's worth holding in mind that Roles that are out of kilter with the OE Spine can be easily mistaken for talent or capability gaps.

b) Common Currents

Have a discussion about the three common organization Currents. Are any of them evident and if so, how do they show up in your organization? Here are a few questions to get you started:

- **Rush Current** – Is there a pervasive pattern of rushing to action? Is there a lot of pressure on deadlines? What interventions are creating noise or cynicism? Could this be a sign of simplistic solutions?
- **Control Current** – Is there a pervasive pattern of control on decision making and permissions? Do you find yourself being asked to opine on or make decisions on lower level or low risk activity? Do people wait for you to tell them what to do next? Are there areas of the business that seem to be holding back the wider system or take more time than other areas to respond and act?
- **Blame Current** – Is there a pervasive pattern of defensive Behaviours that shows up in multiple places? Do you experience people passing the buck or complaining about other people or areas? More subtly, do you find people being careful with their words, which leaves you none the wiser?

Once you've generated the initial list of possible OE issues from your discussions, the next step is to estimate which ones are costing you the most money and causing the most pain – regardless of how hard they might be to tackle. You're starting to prioritize the issues you're going to go after first. Candidly, the issues that need addressing the most, repeatedly get blindsided and continue to hide cost and hold stress in the system. This is the strength of the system pushing back. This is where you need to hold your nerve, be 'willing and able' and select the challenging issues as the focus of a full 3D-OE Diagnostic.

- ***Step 1 Outcome: Prioritized list of OE issues that are hampering performance.***

Step 2 – Framing your OE question

As soon as you ask a question, the status quo will start to shift because it raises awareness of the issue and people begin to think about it.

This is a 'go slow, to go fast' *moment*. How the OE question is framed is significant because it will influence the direction of the change. In our 3D-OE Diagnostic Model, alignment of the central OE Spine is what you are striving for. The OE question you articulate puts boundaries round the scope of the Diagnostic and becomes the North Star through the Process. Framing the OE question also begins to engage 'hearts and minds' so that people start noticing the issue.

Hallmarks of a strong OE question:

- Aligned to and in service of the Vision & Strategy of the business.

- Use straightforward language – so a bright 11-year-old would understand it.
- Targeted to the extent that it is clear where the edges are – clarity about what is in scope and what is not.
- Tangible so that when you move to action it is easier to measure progress and outcomes.

This could be framed up as an outcome (we want to accelerate…) or as a question (how do we improve…?).

- ***Step 2 Outcome: Strong OE question that will frame the scope of the Diagnostic and the work beyond***

Step 3 – Gathering Data

It's important to approach gathering your data in a particular way to get the most out of the 3D-OE Diagnostic Framework™. Whilst you are likely to have lots of sources of data which will provide valuable insight, the Diagnostic is an anthropological approach. It relies on the involvement of your colleagues. The best way forward is to create a group – your cohort – using the three principles below. When you do this, you *leverage* the ambiguous reality of your organizations and engage 'hearts and minds' from the outset. The cohort will provide insights into your specific OE question and their early engagement means they are more likely to support you when it comes to identifying and implementing actions.

- **Multiple perspectives** – It is vital to draw on perspectives from a wide range of people, each bringing their own frames of reference. The cohort needs to include both supporters and detractors. An organizational anthropological approach offers deep insight into social systems, past and present – how people live, think and organize themselves, and why those differences matter. By tapping into the organization as a living system, we can uncover how individuals perceive its functioning and, just as importantly, how they experience life within it.

- **Expertise** – Expertise already exists within the business – it's simply spread across different functions, disciplines and Roles. By engaging with people from many parts of the organization and connecting their knowledge, you begin to weave together a more complete picture. This collective insight not only frames the issues more clearly but also shapes solutions in a richer, more rounded way. The issues and the solutions are *already known* to the people in the business, you just have to find them and listen to them and join the dots.
- **Fractals** – To truly understand an organization, it's important to listen to voices from across the spectrum – different levels, experiences and Roles. This breadth of perspective allows you to harness the fractal nature of organizations. A fractal is a mathematical pattern in which each part mirrors the whole. In the same way, fractal management theory suggests that as individuals attune to their organizational system, they become reflections of it.[1] By asking enough people the same questions, you begin to see repeating patterns

emerge. These common threads provide a consistent and accurate view of what is happening across the entire organization, enabling deeper insight and more grounded analysis.

Recommendation for data collection

Once you've selected your diagnostic cohort against the three principles above you will need to organize forums for gathering data – we use 1–1 conversations and small focus groups. These can be conducted face to face or virtually. You are aiming for the kind of open, curious non-leading conversations anthropologists use in the field. These conversations are characterized by:

- Keeping within the parameters of *your* OE question.
- Using open questions.
- Participant led story telling.
- Deep listening – especially listening without interpretation to stay as neutral as possible, even if you don't agree.
- Minimal interference including not interrupting.
- Pay attention to context, meaning and lived experience.
- Write down exactly what people say including quotes – it helps to increase trust and openness in the conversation if you are seen to write rather than using technology to record or transcribe, as this can limit what people are prepared to say.

- ***Step 3 Outcome: Rich and extensive data and insights from your diagnostic cohort***

Step 4 – Analysing your data through the 3D-OE Model

There are lots of ways you can analyse the data from your conversations. Below is our four-point formula. We've found this is the best way to make sense of the data that you've gathered.

1. **Data analysis round 1** – Topic identification
    - Look across the data to identify repeating words, ideas and phrases that show up sprinkled through the data and categorize them into topics that are common to the majority of the diagnostic cohort.
    - Be on alert for data that is camouflaging the true nature of the situation and holding the status quo in place.
    - If data is limited to a single person's view, however valid, we recommend it is omitted. You are looking for a systemic viewpoint, and it is important to ensure that personal agendas don't influence the findings.
2. **Data analysis round 2** – Mine the data and map it to the topics.

3. **Data analysis round 3** – Organize the data under each topic against the four elements of the 3D-OE Diagnostic Model. This must be done in a specific way to unlock increasing levels of complexity. Using AI to help sift through and organize *anonymized* data – personal or company – can streamline this round.

   - Always start with Roles, then Traversals, then Fault Lines and finally Currents.
   - Notice the Constructs, then Behaviours and notice the themes and patterns that are an indication of Interplays.
   - The accumulated (repeating) Interplays will give you clues to the Currents.
   - Each data point can be allocated to more than one of the four dynamic elements of the Model. This helps to illuminate the layers of complexity.

4. **Reporting your findings** – As you start to report your findings, again work in the specific order we've shared: Roles, Traversals, Fault Lines and Currents. This enables you to present your insights at each level of complexity and facilitates a 3D perspective on the issue.

   - Plan to write a document not a slide deck.
   - Refer to the detailed chapters on the Diagnostic Model including the six principles around

Roles, nature of Traversals, understanding Fault Lines and how to think about the influence of Currents.

- To preserve detail and the flow of ideas summarize your findings in full sentences and structured paragraphs – this allows for nuances, explanation and context. Wherever possible use direct quotes to enrich the insight. Make sure you don't attribute quotes to a person or include a quote that is easily identifiable.
- Words matter – be clear what you mean by the words you use because they can distract people from making sense and lead to misinterpretation.
- At this stage it's vital not to lose the richness of the insights by truncating people's words into bullet points or shorthand key words – leave them as they are, even if that means lots of text on the page. Doing it this way preserves the original meaning.
- Pay attention to legal, privacy and ethical considerations – these may be best omitted from the report and shared through the appropriate channels.
- Write it as you heard it – be *willing and able* to not shy away from reporting it as it is, don't filter the information because of fears about

being 'shot as the messenger' or attempt to spin it to something more positive than it is. Say it as it is – share the reality of the organization.

- A final note on the report of findings. We believe it is important not to muddy the waters by seeking to validate the accuracy of the data, *provided* you followed the three principles outlined in step 3. The data is a collective perception and experience of life in your system.

You might be wondering why we've placed so much emphasis on *how* the report is written. It's principally because the default practice in organizations is to produce slide decks. We advocate writing the report as a document not a slide presentation because corporate-style slide templates inevitably impose a linear, compressed and overly tidy structure which glosses over the reality of OE issues. Slide decks can give the impression that the solutions are simple, when in reality you're focusing on situations which are complex, interconnected and full of nuance.

▶ ***Step 4 Outcome: 3D-OE Diagnostic Report – the examined reality of your organization***

Chapter 10
Making sense of your organization effectiveness issues

We've laid out our Process for using the 3D-OE Diagnostic Framework™ and by using it you will have examined your system. However, without pausing to allow sufficient time for all relevant stakeholders and participants to make sense of the findings, this will be just another report. You now need to be *willing and able to hold people in the diagnostic space* and keep going with the Process. The conversations have happened and the report has been written but no-one has had time yet to digest and understand the findings. Your Role, at this stage, is to help your stakeholders make sense of the systemic viewpoints and the aggregation of themes captured in the report. This will take time as everyone else will still be in their existing frames of reference and seeing things from their part of the organization. This is a period between doing the Diagnostic and moving into action – it's critical to avoid the Rush Current and risk implementing simplistic solutions.

What is sense-making?

For humans, sense-making is an existential psychological need. We will do this no matter what, even without all the available information. Our brains jump to conclusions because they evolved for speed rather than accuracy. Human brains use a lot of energy. An adult brain consumes around 20% of the body's total energy despite making up only around 2% of body weight.[1] We automatically take short cuts by filling in gaps in the available information to conserve effort. We also prefer the simplest coherent story to avoid having to stay in uncertainty for too long. As we covered in Chapter 3, jumping to conclusions gives us a sense of control and the emotional safety we seek.

The definition of sense-making is the process by which people create plausible interpretations and make sense of their experience and create meaning from ambiguous, uncertain or complex situations.[2]

Sense-making is often confused or conflated with communicating. Communication is a classic 'Rush Current' in many organizations. Even good communication is selective as you choose what to say, what to leave out and how to position messages. Communicating is often about simplifying a message so that the greatest number of people understand it in the same way. In this sense you are *reducing* ambiguity rather than *leveraging* it. Relying on communication alone risks missing out on this key stage.

We recommend you share the Report without redactions. You are after all playing back what people have said and what they already know. This is the moment you bring your rotten fish out into the open and prevent them festering any further. However, you need to use your judgement about how you share any particularly sensitive people issues that may have been named or where there may be potential legal implications.

If you follow our principles for writing the Diagnostic Report, you will have a rich and comprehensive document. Because it is written in full sentences and paragraphs, supported by actual quotes, it's likely to be longer than people are used to reading in a work setting. It might be more like reading a short novel – evocative, immersive and likely to surface emotions and areas of disagreement. An enriching read and well worth the time.

The 3D-OE Diagnostic Report is intended to deliberately and transparently 'speak truth to power' by describing the common themes named by the diagnostic cohort. They may be uncomfortable truths and at this stage may raise more questions than answers.

Why is sense-making important?

The point of making sense of the Diagnostic is to align on what it means so that there is shared understanding across all your stakeholders. Everyone needs to have the opportunity to be clear about the reality of the organization, warts and all.

This alignment enables clear choices to be made about how to shift the status quo and solve the OE issues.

This is always easier said than done and not everybody will be able to align with some or all of the findings or it may just take them time. Some people will quickly want to get to an interpretation that is plausible. Plausibility here means that they reach a viewpoint that is believable to them and seems reasonable but may not be the reality of the organization. In this case, people may not be ready to widen their frames of reference. Others may cut corners to reduce ambiguity, for example, by not reading the report or by reading it but picking out aspects that reinforce their current frames of reference.

Building shared understanding around the Diagnostic findings is about teasing out how people are interpreting the information, considering differences and working out where everyone is coming from. This is *how* you are leveraging ambiguity. It's not about reaching consensus where everybody agrees with each other. It's about generating mutual clarity and shared comprehension of all the perspectives in the Report. It is about active listening, open mindedness and mutual candour – engaging *hearts and minds*. Shared understanding is the game changer.

Sense-making approaches

As a leader, your Role at this stage is to be the 'honest broker' by facilitating a process that enables all the stakeholders to understand the perspectives of the diagnostic cohort.

Sharing the 3D-OE Diagnostic Report

When you are thinking about who all the stakeholders are, it's important that you think about the Roles and people that you need onside or aware as you begin to move towards solutions. The diagnostic cohort is part of your stakeholder group.

When considering the cohort, you may not be used to sharing insight quite so openly – most of the time we are communicating as we described above. But if you followed our principles for gathering data, you will have chosen people because you wanted to hear their voices – it's wise to honour this. You have also begun the process of winning hearts and minds – the status quo will have started to shift. This is a delicate time when you can erode all the goodwill that you will have gained by including people in the Diagnostic Process. It's important to continue to engage them on the journey.

We would always recommend that you send the whole Report to all stakeholders – this level of transparency builds the trust you need to solve your complex OE issues.

Building shared understanding

Sending out the Report to your stakeholders is the first step. However, this alone is not sufficient to enable proper sense-making and get the most value out of the investment of time and effort in the Diagnostic Process.

Here's a brief explanation of the two conditions which you need to plan for and enable.

1. **Time**
   It is really important that you allocate enough time for this stage. At this point the Rush Current will be kicking in and even if you are comfortable it is likely that you will be under pressure to jump to an action plan to implement solutions. There is no hard and fast rule about how long this takes, but you need to allow a good block of time for people to read, digest and process the information. This is not a one-off email that communicates the story so far.

2. **Opportunity**
   You need to use existing forums and perhaps provide new forums, workshops and channels for people to discuss the Diagnostic Report and ask questions or pose challenges *without* fear of judgement. Ideally you can use these opportunities to cross-fertilize sense-making. In other words, use the workshops and forums to encourage active listening, join up across different perspectives, link across boundaries and share, clarify and understand interpretations.

Our recommendation would be to repeat and revisit these activities until there are enough people or enough of the right people who share a common understanding.

You are aiming to reach a turning point where the nature of the issues is sufficiently and widely understood so that those with the power to accelerate the shift in the status quo can start to make decisions and determine actions that will address the OE issues.

We acknowledge the sense-making approach we are recommending is orientated to national cultures that lean towards brainstorming and see discussion and conflict as a part of problem solving. In high power or deferential cultures decisions often rest with senior leaders and therefore what we are recommending may feel risky. One common approach in contexts such as these is to overtly set a principle and a boundary that for the duration of the forum the hierarchy is temporarily suspended but then resumes when people leave the discussion.

Moving to action

As no two organizations are the same, the effectiveness issues you encounter will naturally differ. It follows, then, that the solutions that will help resolve your issues will be as varied. There are numerous, high quality, innovative solutions to OE issues of all kinds. As we've discussed, they will only deliver value and avoid becoming simplistic when they're shaped by a true grasp of what's really going on in your unique context. Whatever solutions you choose must work on both Constructs and Behaviours in an interdependent way. The mutual reliance of the solutions ensures new Constructs and Behaviours reinforce one another to create meaningful shifts in your organization's Interplays.

As you move through the Diagnostic process from data gathering to analysis to sense-making you will have unlocked the layers of complexity, gained deep insight, identified tangible places to start and developed the aligned cohort of stakeholders who are now ready to face into the knotty organization issues hiding cost.

The advantage of the effectiveness edge

In a business context the term 'edge' refers to a discernible competitive advantage created from favourable internal conditions. From an OE perspective this is when you've spotted and dealt with the kinks in your OE Spine and your organization's resources – both money and people – are optimally aligned. We've all had experiences of being part of a team or project when work flows more easily, day-to-day operations run smoothly and people are positive, energized and productive. This is when hidden cost is at its minimum and that part of the organization is most effective.

Throughout this book, our clear intention has been to paint the reality of organizations and, despite that reality, encourage you to face into your OE issues. We've offered you a clear and accessible way to put your 'fish on the table' – so you will always have a way to identify what isn't working as well as it could. We've advocated throughout the need to 'go slow, to go fast'. This is critically important and fundamental to creating an effective internal environment. It takes time to understand the true nature of OE issues – to diagnose before action, to look at the organization up, down and across, to spend time sense-making and to avoid simplistic solutions that simply perpetuate costs.

We've aimed to put the discipline of OE at the forefront of your mind and the top of your to-do list. If you want the discernable commercial advantage OE can bring, it can't be optional. The discipline of OE, encapsulated in the 3D-OE Diagnostic Framework, has to be an expectation on all your leaders. You need to be willing and able to use our approach to cut through complexity and sharpen your insight to make confident OE decisions.

Most organizations are ineffective. Now you've read this book, yours doesn't have to be.

Notes

Introduction

[1] Kohlrieser, G., Goldsworthy, S., & Coombe, D. *Hostage at the Table: How leaders can overcome conflict, influence others, and raise performance* (2012). Story adapted from George Kohlrieser's metaphor, which describes how unaddressed issues, like fish left under the table, begin to rot and drive people away.

[2] Comprehensive list of Constructs and Behaviours.

Examples of organization Constructs:

- Organization structures such as Roles and organization charts.
- Organizational boundaries including those that are showing up as Fault Lines, both internal and external.
- Anything that might create a principle, guideline, guardrail or definable edge or practice in the system.
- Control systems, such as policies and frameworks.
- Organization processes.
- Legal contracts and business agreements.
- Defined levels of authority.
- Governance protocols.
- Leadership systems, including which Roles can make decisions or are designated with membership of leadership teams and committees.
- Formal and informal meetings.
- Any principle or boundary that defines and organizes groups.
- Physical locations, design of spaces and seating arrangements.

- Symbols such as brands, websites, fonts, colours.

Examples of Behaviours:

- Individual action or non-action.
- What people say and don't say.
- What people pay attention to and focus on.
- What people ignore, blindside or overlook.
- Relationships between people including alliances, affiliations and support.
- Unconscious reactions.
- Conscious responses.
- Facial expressions.
- Gestures including body language.
- Power dynamics.
- Team dynamics.
- Rituals, habits, routines and traditions.

[3] Berne, E. *The Structure and Dynamics of Organizations and Groups* (1963) and Napper, R. *The DNA Model* (n.d.). Building on Rosemary Napper's extensive organizational Transactional Analysis thinking, based on Berne's original work, the DNA model is a practitioner framework that illustrates how organization structures and behavioural dynamics interact to shape culture.

Part 1

Chapter 1

[1] Aristotle, *History of Animals*, trans. D'Arcy Wentworth Thompson, Book IV, Part 1 (1910).

[2] Erikson, E. H. *Identity: Youth and crisis* (1968) and Levin, P. *Becoming The Way We Are: A transactional guide to personal development* (1974).

[3] Rooke, D. & Torbert, W. R. *Seven Transformations of Leadership.* Harvard Business Review, 83(4), 67–76 (2005). Constructive adult development theories describe how adults construct meaning – and how that meaning-making capacity can develop through qualitatively different stages over time. Development here is not about acquiring greater skill or knowledge (horizontal development), but about transforming the underlying way experience is interpreted (vertical development). Rooke and Torbert apply this lens to leadership. Their central argument is that what differentiates leaders is not personality, style, or philosophy, but

their internal 'action logic' – a person's dominant way of making sense of reality, exercising power, relating to others, and taking responsibility.

[4] This statistic is derived from Harthill Consulting's Profiling process using their renowned Leadership Development Profile. This was shared with the authors directly: 'Of the 16,500+ leaders, coaches and consultants profiled by Harthill Consulting in the past 25 years, 57% profiled at Achiever [Action Logic] (all three sub-stages included)'.

[5] This paragraph describes someone who is moving from Achiever to Individualist Action Logic. The blend illustrates both the value of these frames of reference and their shadow side. To further illuminate this, here are Harthill's descriptions of leadership shaped by each Action Logic.

a. Achiever Action Logic. Achiever is a creative initiator – future-oriented, driven, adaptable and results-focused. They seek ways around problems to deliver the desired outcome, welcome behavioural feedback and appreciate complexity and systems thinking. They pursue increasing mutuality in relationships and are genuinely reflective. Their shadow side is limited insight into the unintended consequences of their strengths, and a tendency toward guilt when they fall short of their own standards. They tend to adopt rather than create major goals, and their orientation is firmly toward effectiveness and mid-term results.
b. Individualist Action Logic. Individualist begins to question the assumptions of self, other and system with deep curiosity. They are more aware of their own shadow and of the flip side to their strengths. There is a shift toward radical inquiry, self-awareness and a felt experience of complexity – an attraction to change, difference and questioning across more domains of life. They work for deep personal relatedness and are increasingly free-thinking, learning to hold deeper tensions for longer. They take on different roles in different situations, though this can bring an authenticity challenge. Their orientation shifts from results toward process, and they begin to live with paradox rather than resolve it. © Harthill Consulting Ltd.

Chapter 2

[1] Spoken by Socrates and recorded by Plato. Plato. *Apology* (38a). In *Plato: Complete works* (c. 399 BCE).

Chapter 3

[1] Reagan, R. *Remarks at a Reception for Members of the Associated General Contractors of America* (1981).
[2] Heraclitus (c. 500 BCE). Fragment, quoted in Plato, *Cratylus* (401d). In J. M. Cooper (Ed.), *Plato: Complete works* (1997).
[3] Cannon, Walter B. *Bodily Changes in Pain, Hunger, Fear and Rage* (1915) and Walker, P. *Complex PTSD: From surviving to thriving* (2013).
[4] LeDoux, J. E. *The Emotional Brain: The mysterious underpinnings of emotional life* (1996) and Sapolsky, R. M. *Why Zebras Don't Get Ulcers* (3rd ed.) (2004).
[5] Heifetz, R. A., Grashow, A., & Linsky, M. *The Practice of Adaptive Leadership: Tools and tactics for changing your organization and the world* (2009).

Part 2

Chapter 4

[1] Attributed to Mahatma Gandhi, sourced from *ABA Journal*, Volume 53, 1011 (November 1967).
[2] Plutarch *Life of Theseus*, 23. In *Parallel Lives*, trans. Bernadotte Perrin. Cambridge (1914). According to Plutarch, when the hero Theseus was returning to Crete after killing the Minotaur, the journey took so long that the ship's wooden planks began to rot. Whenever this happened the Athenians replaced the decaying planks with new timber, one-by-one. By the end of the journey, every original part of the ship had been replaced.

Chapter 5

[1] Schmid, B. *Transactional Analysis and Social Roles* in The Maastricht Papers: Selected papers from the 20th EATA Conference, 30–44 (July 1994).

Chapter 6

[1] Soda, G., Iorio, A., & Rizzo, L. *In the Network of the Conclave: Social connections and the making of a pope* in Social Networks, 83, 215–232 (2025).
[2] Camilleri, T., Rockey, S., & Dunbar, R. *The Social Brain: The psychology of successful groups* (2023).

Part 3

Chapter 9

[1] Henderson, T. L. & Boje, D. M. *Organizational Development and Change Theory: Managing fractal organising processes* (2015).

Chapter 10

[1] Balasubramanian, V. *Brain power* in Proceedings of the National Academy of Sciences, 118(32), e2107022118 (2021).
[2] Weick, K. E. *Sensemaking in Organizations* (1995) and Weick, K. E., Sutcliffe, K. M., & Obstfeld, D. *Organizing and the Process of Sensemaking in Organization Science*, 16(4), 409–421 (2005).

Further resources

For further resources please head to our website www.theeffectivenessedge.com or scan the QR code below.

Keep up with the latest by following us on Instagram @theeffectivenessedge

Acknowledgements

Vanessa

I have wanted to write this book for a long time – to share what I've learned from the years I've spent living and working in organizations. Yet it was only when I met Andrea, my remarkably accomplished, indomitable co-author and friend, that this long-held ambition became a reality. Finding someone who so deeply understands how I think and see the world and at the same time brings such different and complimentary perspectives, is rare indeed. Working with you, Andrea, is a genuine joy. It has, as we've both said, been a blast!

This book grew out of the many chances I've had to learn, firsthand, how organizations really tick. Along the way, I've been fortunate to work for inspiring bosses, with strong leaders and clients and alongside capable and supportive colleagues. You encouraged me to pivot into OE all those years ago, invested in my professional education and enabled me to build and apply my expertise. I'm grateful for the faith you placed in me.

I've also developed through the guidance and insight of superb teachers and my fellow practitioners – academically, in my personal development, in Transactional Analysis and in my creative fields. Each of you has helped shape who I am and influenced what I want to say in this book.

And to my friends – my favourite people – thank you for your honesty, kindness, generosity and the trust we share. You are truly special.

Yet, none of this would have been possible without the love, support and resilience of my parents, my family, my husband and my sons. You are my roots and my branches. You sustain me.

The final word goes to Lola – small and furry, loud and barky – my constant companion throughout the creation of this book.

Andrea

For over 20 years I've had the quiet ambition to share the insights gathered from a corporate career that has been nothing short of enriching. I've worked with and for many extraordinary people, been given countless opportunities to grow and learned lessons that felt too valuable to leave in the back of my mind. I've had a couple of false starts on the writing front, but life, work and the usual swirl of priorities meant the writing never quite took off.

A few years ago I finally carved out the time to begin. I interviewed a number of people on the topic of accountability, and their stories, honesty and wisdom did something important: they cemented my ambition. They made the book feel not just desirable, but necessary. Their insights gave shape to something I'd been thinking about for years. And then I met my co-author Vanessa.

We were genuinely lucky to be paired together in a senior job share – two halves of the same OE Role. What could have been a logistical arrangement became something far richer: a partnership, a shared curiosity and a sense that we were seeing the same organizational patterns from two angles at once. It was the spark that turned intention into momentum. And here we are!

I'm deeply grateful for the partnership of someone whose erudite, intellectual depth consistently sharpened my thinking. Working with her on this book was not only stimulating but genuinely fun. Her willingness to explore new angles, challenge assumptions and laugh along the way made the work richer and very rewarding. It's been a blast… book 2?

For all the years I've been toying with the idea there have been two people who never wavered. My husband and my mother.

Both of them backed me from the very beginning. Not once did they roll their eyes or suggest it was a foolish idea. They quite simply believed I had something to offer. That kind of belief is a gift, and it carried me further than they probably realize. Thank you both. You are amazing. I couldn't have done it without you.

And then there's my daughter, whose pride in her mum has been its own kind of fuel. She has this way of making me feel like what I'm doing matters, like it's worth the effort, worth the courage it takes to put something into the world.

Last but by no means least, a huge thank you to all those friends and colleagues who have encouraged me along the way. I am deeply grateful for your support and friendship.

Together

There are a number of people we'd like to both thank who have been instrumental in getting this book onto the shelf.

Our beta readers who gave up their weekends and spare time to read our draft manuscript. They placed their trust in us, confident we wouldn't waste their time and gave us pearls of wisdom and feedback that undeniably shaped the book into something far better. Thank you Faye Frater, Andrew Gibson, Jen Johnston, Samantha Rockey, Emma Rose, Victoria Stone, Gareth Turney, Penny Young and Ruth D'Rozario from Practical Inspiration Publishing.

We've had the benefit of valuable insight and knowledge from Elaine Grix, Innes Murray, Charles Robottom and David Rooke. Thank you all.

We'd like to acknowledge the significant contribution of the Practical Inspiration Publishing team for their support, the cover design and illustrations, the navigation through the publishing process and getting the book out there into the real world.

Last but by no means least, to Alison Jones – for spotting the potential of the book, pivotal advice at key points and practical guidance. Thank you for believing in us and recognizing we have something to say.

About the authors

Vanessa Loughlin is a trusted specialist in organization effectiveness with a clear view: most organizations aren't held back by strategy, but by the way they're designed to work. Founder of Organisation Matters Ltd, she partners with CEOs and executive teams to understand issues, surface hidden costs and make organization decisions that create competitive advantage. With 35 years experience across global businesses including Motorola, Vodafone, Barclays and Aviva, she specializes in diagnosing and resolving complex issues to unlock organization, team and individual performance. A systems thinker and straight talker – guided by clarity over complexity, truth over comfort and impact over activity. She co-authored *The Effectiveness Edge: How Organization Effectiveness Unlocks Performance* with Andrea Robottom – a partnership forged through a job share at Standard Life. Vanessa holds an MSc in Organisation Consulting and is a Fellow of the CIPD. Outside work, she finds balance in family life, long walks with her dog and painting.

Andrea Robottom is a leading voice in organization effectiveness – the person leaders call when they have a business performance issue and the cause is elusive. Known for her candour, clarity and ability to cut through complexity, she helps CEOs and senior executives identify what is truly blocking performance – then act on it. Andrea founded NoNonsense Consulting in 2009 and has over 35 years of global organization effectiveness experience across FMCG, beer, financial services, med tech, retail, utilities, hospitality and not-for-profit. Her corporate career spans Cadbury, PepsiCo, Seagram and Compaq. She is the co-author of *The Effectiveness Edge: How Organization Effectiveness Unlocks Performance* – written with her former job share partner Vanessa Loughlin – which introduces the 3D-OE Diagnostic Framework™. Andrea is an accredited Mediator, Fellow of the CIPD, and Trustee of Precious Sisters, a charity supporting girls' education in Kenya. Outside of work she loves tennis, family games, cooking and exploring the world with her family.

Contact the authors at www.theeffectivenessedge.com

Index

Entries in *italics* refer to figures. Entries of the form *XnY* refer to note Y on page X.

A quick word from Practical Inspiration Publishing...

We hope you found this book both practical and inspiring – that's what we aim for with every book we publish.

We publish titles on topics ranging from leadership, entrepreneurship, HR and marketing to self-development and wellbeing.

Find details of all our books at: www.practicalinspiration.com

Did you know...

We can offer discounts on bulk sales of all our titles – ideal if you want to use them for training purposes, corporate giveaways or simply because you feel these ideas deserve to be shared with your network.

We can even produce bespoke versions of our books, for example with your organization's logo and/or a tailored foreword.

To discuss further, contact us on info@practicalinspiration.com.

Got an idea for a business book?

We may be able to help. Find out about more about publishing in partnership with us at: bit.ly/PIpublishing.

Follow us on social media...

@pip_talking

@practicalinspiration

@piptalking

Practical Inspiration Publishing

www.ingramcontent.com/pod-product-compliance
Lightning Source LLC
LaVergne TN
LVHW102045161026
850310LV00030B/173
* 9 7 8 1 8 0 5 7 6 0 2 8 3 *